God's Remedy for Depression

Vivian Clark

Baker Book House
Grand Rapids, Michigan 49506

ISBN: 0-8010-2444-7
Copyright 1980 by
Baker Book House Company

Printed in the United States of America

SECOND PRINTING, MAY 1981

To Dave,
who, with love and encouragement,
walked with me through the experiences
that produced this book.

CONTENTS

INTRODUCTION

"God, I'm stumbling through a dark hallway and I must find my own way. Darkness hides the doorways. Plaster falls in my eyes as cold wind whines through broken slats. Glass and debris trip my feet. I feel terribly alone and lost. I am depressed!"

Pushing the vacuum cleaner aimlessly over the red shag rug in our family room, a sense of worthlessness overwhelmed me. I was depressed! What was the point in continuing to live? As my emotions sank lower than the carpet I was cleaning, I heard the still small voice of God in my heart.

"Vivian, I'm not finished with you yet. You have a husband who loves you, two boys who need you, and, besides, you're not finished with that book."

As my thoughts turned upward from morbid introspection and focused on God's message to me, my emotions also rose to a level of song and praise to God.

Library shelves are stacked with volumes on the psychology of depression. Religious authors too, struggle to understand and provide answers for this complicated and painful malady. But it is not my purpose to present an intellectual treatise on the psychological aspect of depression. I wrote this book for several reasons.

First of all, in my battles with depression, I found many books on the market unhelpful, frustrating, and *depressing!* If Jesus Christ is actually the Wonderful Counselor spoken of in Isaiah 9:6, then surely He could give me insight from the Scriptures. So I studied to see what God had to say on the subject.

Second, in reading *Satan Is Alive and Well on Planet Earth* by Hal Lindsey, a comment burned itself into my thinking.

When Jesus told us we are to be 'in the world but not of it,' He meant that we are not to cop out or drop out but to reject the world's hold on our affections and mental attitudes. Then we can be part of the solution for the world instead of part of the problem.

We need more Christian writers, artists, business people, and educators who will produce works that express God's viewpoint. This is not a time for withdrawal; this is a time for involvement![1]

His words challenged me to see if the common problem of depression could be dealt with in a biblical way, rather than following the humanistic approach of modern psychology or psychiatry.

Last, I wrote to share with countless others in my world that Jesus Christ is indeed the Wonderful Counselor. I have found victory in Him over that dreary enemy, Depression, stalking about and waiting for a chance to capture me and toss me over the cliff of despair.

First we need to briefly answer some questions: What is depression? What causes depression? And who becomes depressed?

WHAT IS DEPRESSION?

Depression is a commonly used word with a variety of meanings. To many it is simply a low mood, lasting a brief time, due perhaps to disappointment or frustration. To others depression is a long duration of a feeling of despair. These victims see no value in living and wish they had never been born. They may even contemplate and pursue suicide.

In his book, *Up From Depression,* Dr. Leonard Cammer portrays the feelings of a depressed person. This person has a

> sense that something is wrong and pulling him down. He will verbalize it: "I have such a heavy heart."
>
> The heavy heart signifies utter weariness. A person in this condition may drag about all day and wonder how to push through it. Or, if the depression is intense, he or she will not get going at all. The sluggishness is plain to be seen as the person bogs down at any little obstacle. His thinking faculties seem dulled and he blanks out in a conversation. At the same time he complains, "I'm so jittery and restless."[2]

A depressed teenager may take no interest in his studies, appear moody and sullen, find nothing challenging to occupy his time. A depressed housewife will drag through breakfast, heaving a weighty sigh when the door closes after her departing family, and she may even go back to bed. The cluttered kitchen makes her feel more depressed, but she lacks the motivation to clean it up. The usually happy and outgoing person becomes quiet and listless when depressed and is unable to join in conversation. He or she cannot appreciate the beauty of sunlight streaming through towering birch trees, or the comical antics of a friendly squirrel.

Depression is accompanied by mental pain which Dr. Cammer describes this way: "This is a unique emotional quality compounded of anguish and despair, self-disgust, and intense guilt with anger and fear. Mental pain may also express itself as agitation and hopelessness. The sufferer wishes that he had never been born or could return to nonexistence."[3]

WHAT CAUSES DEPRESSION?

Causes of depression are varied and many. Some authors seek to simplify these by forming two main categories—anger and self-pity. Others write long lists of causes, each to be treated in a different way. In any case, we must realize that there is both a general and specific cause for depression.

General Cause

The general cause for depression is a condition of the flesh, or of the self-life. Walking after the flesh, or living the self-life, occurs any time I do not actively choose to walk in the Spirit, or to surrender to His control. "This I say then, Walk in the Spirit, and ye shall not fulfill the lust of the flesh" (Gal. 5:16, KJV).

Paul described the works of the flesh in Galatians 5:17-21. Depression may be included in the phrase "and such like," since it certainly isn't an evidence of the fruit of the Spirit listed in Galatians 5:22, 23. In the case of depression this is *usually* an involuntary response based on past conditioning—the repetitious groove cut into the record of the mind and emotions. I say *usually* because there are few people who choose to be depressed. There may be some who use this problem to relieve themselves of undesirable responsibility or to manipulate others to pamper them or meet their emotional needs. However, this has not been my experience.

Depression has always been, for me, an automatic response to stress or disappointment. Before I had time to think or prevent it from happening, I was smothered under its heavy blanket. Then, by the very nature of depression, I would lack motivation or ability to pull myself "out of it."

I am not excusing the response, but only wish to explain it at this point. The concluding chapter explains in detail freedom from the bondage of depression, which is available in Jesus Christ.

Specific Causes

Specific causes for depression may be any number of things; deceptions, fatigue, pressure, satanic oppression, rejection, poor self-concept, grief, physical illness. The precipitating factors, or circumstances, behind depression can be as varied as the individuals who experience depression.

Depression is only a symptom of a deeper problem, not the disease in and of itself. To illustrate, think of a child sick with a fever. We may treat the problem with aspirin and cool baths, reducing the temperature temporarily. However, if a disease or bacteria is causing the fever, it will return and become increasingly higher. The real *cause* of the fever needs to be determined by blood tests, throat cultures, spinal taps, or whatever accompanying symptoms indicate.

Likewise, depression must be regarded only as a symptom. To treat it with anti-depressants, psychotherapy, or even spiritual formulas— "confess it as sin," "take it to the cross," or "claim your victory,"—may alleviate the symptoms temporarily. However, it is necessary to uncover and deal with the cause in order to bring lasting freedom.

WHO BECOMES DEPRESSED?

I cannot answer this question without looking at some basic temperament differences in individuals. I believe we are born with our temperaments—the subconscious part of our beings over which the conscious mind has little control. Temperament is that stamp of individuality demonstrated in every human creation, causing us to react in different ways to our environment.

Hallesby, in his book *Temperament and the Christian Faith,* describes it:

> Like water flowing from a spring, taking its color and iron from sources deep down in the earth; and all the water gushing from this one spring is of the same nature. But when it comes out into the open, then we can decide whether or not to make use of it, what we shall use it for, whether we want to use it as it is or add something to it to improve its quality.[4]

He adds, "Temperament has to do only with the functioning of the soul-life. It strikes the key or chord to which the soul must vibrate. It gives the tempo which will control the natural rhythm of soul and body."[5]

This truth was demonstrated in our youngest son. By the time he was two years old we knew we had a temperament on our hands which needed to be treated with special sensitivity.

"Did you have a good time in Sunday school?"

"My teacher wouldn't let me sing."

Or, "She made me sit in a chair," he would respond in a mournful tone.

He inherited this temperament quite naturally. I look at my ancestors and see poets, musicians, and artists, but people filled with depression and anxiety. Out of eight children in my family, at least two of us inherited the same traits.

My son and I always see the negative side before the positive, the problems and the defects. My husband can look at the newly mown back yard with satisfaction and approval, and say, "Doesn't it look nice?" But I see all the weeds in the beds around the fence, the thistles coming out of the rocks and think, "What a mess!"

This type of person hurts over things for a long time—things other people don't even see or feel, or if they do, they shrug off as unimportant. His perfectionism makes it difficult to be satisfied with himself or anyone else. The self-life manifests itself in depression to a greater degree in the person with this temperament.

Throughout this book I wish to examine the lives of interesting people whose experiences with depression are recorded in the Bible. Causes will be noted, and God's remedy examined. In conclusion, depression as a symptom of the self-life will be dealt with from a New Testament perspective.

We will find Elijah sitting under the juniper

tree, tired and longing to die; walk with Naomi along the dusty road back to Bethlehem and share her sorrow and bitterness; weep with Jeremiah over the destruction of his beloved city; visit Job on his ash heap, scraping his boils and bemoaning his birth and life; listen to the prayer of Hannah as she pours out the agony of her soul to God in the temple; and stand appalled at the unreasonable depression of Jonah, whining under the dying gourd. We will find Moses in the desert pleading his cause before God, overwhelmed with his heavy burden.

Each person had one basic cause triggering depression, complicated by accompanying negative factors. Elijah suffered the consequences of his implusive behavior. Naomi's depression resulted from grief. Jeremiah was bound with feelings of rejection. Job experienced satanic oppression and harassment unlike any other person recorded in Scripture. Hannah's depression anchored into frustrated goals, while Jonah retained blatant, unconfessed sin in his life. And Moses was burdened with job pressure.

In examining the lives of these individuals, each of whom God loved and with whom He met personally, we will answer four pertinent questions. What are the circumstances leading up to the depressive state? What are the causes for the depression? What does God's encounter with the depressed teach us about treatment? And finally, what are the results of the encounter in the person's life?

It is my desire that as you read this book you will become acquainted with each individual as a person, understanding his background and personality, and identifying with the problems causing his depression. I want you to see God in a new way, as intensely loving and kind, yet firm and helpful. I hope you will have a greater ability to understand and deal with depression in your own life or in helping a relative or friend by applying God's principles. Most of all, I want you to learn to turn to God, the great counselor and comforter, the only source of ultimate and complete healing for depression.

---

1. Hal Lindsey, *Satan Is Alive and Well on Planet Earth* (Grand Rapids: Zondervan, 1972), p. 112.
2. Leonard Cammer, *Up From Depression* (New York: Simon and Schuster, 1969), pp. 17, 18.
3. Ibid., p. 18.
4. O. Hallesby, *Temperament and the Christian Faith* (Minneapolis: Augsburg, 1978), p. 6.
5. Ibid., p. 7.

1

IMPULSIVE BEHAVIOR
℞: Elijah

Under the rule of wicked King Ahab, Israel reveled in lust and idolatry. His beautiful but unscrupulous, cruel and licentious Queen Jezebel had led the nation in Baal worship. The high places—groves in the hills—attracted worshipers, coming and going, to engage in the evil rites and orgies of this religion. Throbbing drums and clanging cymbals muted the screams of innocent children being sacrificed to this cruel god who is no god. It is recorded that "Ahab did more to provoke the Lord God of Israel . . . than all the kings of Israel who were before him" (I Kings 16:33).

Into this bleak scene stepped Elijah. Into the king's court, uninvited, he strode. What boldness and courage! The glint of fire burned in his eyes! Purpose and determination guided him across the polished marble floor. His voice, deep and strong, echoed through the great hall. "As the Lord the God of Israel lives, before whom I stand, there shall be neither dew nor rain these years, except by my word" (I Kings 17:1). And as lightning streaks through the stormy sky, Elijah was gone.

And it didn't rain. All Israel murmured Elijah's name—first with awe, respect, and courage, but soon with hatred, bitterness, and vengeance. It didn't rain. And all Israel dried under the scorching sun; the trees drooped in despair. The song of the brooks faded into a mournful trickle and disappeared. The physical appearance of the land reflected the hopelessness of the Israelites' spiritual drought. Baal, god of the land and provider of rain and crops, failed. But greater failure permeated the hearts of the people who refused to return to their true Creator-God.

God took care of His obedient prophet. Elijah knew the special care and tenderness of a loving Father as he drank from the brook Cherith and ate bread and meat delivered by the ravens. And surely Elijah was also refreshed spiritually as days passed. What fellowship he must have enjoyed as he waited for God's direction! Certainly he found assurance for his doubts. "Is God really working in this famine?" "Does He have something else for me to do?"

He learned patience in his restlessness, comfort in his loneliness, so that when the last trickle in the brook became only a damp reminder in the sand and disappeared, Elijah was prepared to follow God to a place of provision and ministry (I Kings 17:2–7).

God directed Elijah to visit the widow of Zarephath. She was poor, with only enough oil and meal to provide one last lunch for her son and herself before they faced death. But when she shared with Elijah, God caused her barrel of meal to be never emptied, and her cruse of oil to never run dry (I Kings 17:8–16).

But again Elijah's faith was tested. The widow's son became sick and died. Never before was there recorded an instance of resurrection from the dead. Nevertheless Elijah cried out to God, stretching himself over the child three times. "And the Lord heard the voice of Elijah, and the life of the child returned to him and he revived" (I Kings 17:22).

Elijah, with faith strengthened, left Zarephath prepared for God's battle with pagan Israel.

For three and one half years the king searched for Elijah. Across barren plains and over parched hills his chariots rumbled, dust blowing mockery in the faces of his men. But in God's perfect timing Elijah appeared to Ahab himself, beginning one of the most dramatic confrontations of all time.

"Now it came about after many days, that the

word of the Lord came to Elijah in the third year, saying, "Go, show yourself to Ahab, and I will send rain on the face of the earth" (I Kings 18:1).

As Elijah sauntered down the dusty trail toward the palace, he met Obadiah, Ahab's chief servant. After persistent persuasion, Obadiah took Elijah's message to his master. "Behold, Elijah is here" (I Kings 18:11).

"And it came about, when Ahab saw Elijah that Ahab said to him, "Is this you, you troubler of Israel?"

"And he said, "I have not troubled Israel, but you and your father's house have, because you have forsaken the commandments of the Lord, and you have followed the Baals. Now then send and gather to me all Israel at Mount Carmel, together with 450 prophets of Baal and 400 prophets of the Asherah, who eat at Jezebel's table" (I Kings 18:17–19).

At the command of Elijah and the king, all the people of Israel and the prophets of Baal trekked to the top of Mount Carmel. Questions and murmurings, excitement and apprehension permeated the moving crowds. At last the majestic voice of the man of God rang out.

"How long will you hesitate between two opinions? If the Lord is God, follow Him; but if Baal, follow him" (I Kings 18:21).

The crowd answered with silence. It was now one man and God pitted against 450 of Baal's prophets.

As the contest began, Baal's prophets built an altar, prepared the bullock for sacrifice, and prayed to Baal for fire. This was a very simple request. After all, was not Baal the god of the atmosphere?

"Baal, hear us! Send us fire!" The silent sky mocked their cries.

Their clamor intensified until pandemonium reigned. Jumping and shrieking, convulsing and groaning, the false prophets besought their god who had no ears to hear. Grim faced and horror stricken, the crowd stood transfixed at the appalling scene. Lances and knives slashed and cut, shredding bodies while the thirsty ground soaked up the blood. Timid women fainted. Terrified children cowered behind their mothers' skirts. Strong men felt nauseated. The man of God stood boldly by.

"Maybe your god is asleep, or gone for a walk. Perhaps he's talking with a friend. Shout louder!" he sarcastically derided.

And when they had raved all day until the evening, "there was no voice, no one answered, and no one paid attention" (I Kings 18:29).

The clamor of the day gave way to a quiet hush, broken only by Elijah's authoritative voice, saying, "Come near to me " (I Kings 18:30).

Everyone watched as Elijah repaired the long-neglected altar of God. With twelve stones representing the twelve tribes of Israel, he built an altar to the Lord, cut up the wood and laid on the sacrifice. As the people listened in amazement, they heard, "Fill four barrels with water and pour it on" (KJV).

Was he mad? Daring not to disobey they journeyed down to the sea, filled the barrels and hauled them back.

"Do it again" commanded Elijah.

"And again."

With a thoroughly saturated sacrifice, water filling the trench, and the time for the evening sacrifice at hand, Elijah prayed. "O Lord, the God of Abraham, Isaac and Israel, today let it be known that Thou art God in Israel, and that I am Thy servant, and that I have done all these things at Thy word" (I Kings 18:36).

Whoosh! "Then fire of the Lord fell, and consumed the burnt offering and the wood and the stones and the dust, and licked up the water that was in the trench" (I Kings 18:38).

A recognition of the person of God always demands renunciation of sin and obedience in action. "And when all the people saw it, they fell on their faces; and they said, "The Lord, He is God; the Lord, He is God" (I Kings 18:39).

The dried-up bed of the brook Kishon became the burial place for Baal's prophets, who were seized and killed.

As the scene closed, the defeated King Ahab raced home for dinner and Elijah climbed to the top of Mount Carmel to pray. Seven times he poured himself out to God for rain. Finally a little cloud appeared, a prelude to overcast darkness and torrential rains.

In the New Testament, James refers to Elijah. "Elijah was a man with a nature like ours, and he prayed earnestly that it might not rain; and it did not rain on the earth for three years and six months. And he prayed again, and the sky poured rain, and the earth produced its fruit" (James 5:17, 18).

Few of us identify with the humanness of Elijah as he challenged the Baal worshipers on Mount Carmel. We haven't called down fire or prayed down rain. Yet James says Elijah was as human as we are. For the person who occasionally or frequently finds himself depressed, our next picture of this great man of God provides a shaft of light in a gloomy tunnel.

STATEMENT OF DEPRESSION

It is hard to believe that this courageous fellow, who withstood all Israel, slew 450 prophets of Baal, and sent the king on his way with the promise of rain, fled for his life at the threat from a single woman. This one and only Jezebel sent Elijah a message.

"You killed my prophets, and now I swear by the gods that I am going to kill you by this time tomorrow night."

The next day Elijah was found sitting under a juniper tree in the wilderness, tired, lonely, hungry, and wishing to die. "It is enough; now O Lord, take my life, for I am not better than my fathers" (I Kings 19:4).

Elijah was depressed!

CAUSES OF ELIJAH'S DEPRESSION

There were several causes for Elijah's depression. His impulsive behavior, precipitated by stress, triggered the depressive downward spiral. He ran and thought later. Associated with this was the cycle of life in which every high is followed by a low. Third, there was a physical factor. He was exhausted! To complicate the problem, he did not think clearly. His thoughts dwelt on circumstances rather than on the Person of God; he had unrealistic expectations for himself: and he compared himself unfavorably with others.

Run Now, Think Later

The first cause for Elijah's depression was his impulsive decision to run. Elijah received Jezebel's message; fear gripped him; and he took off for the wilderness. Later, as he introspected under his juniper tree he thought, "What a coward I am! I am no good for anything." And he became depressed.

The depressive person is often an impulsive person. He reacts to his environment impetuously, rather than dealing rationally with circumstances. A decision made instantaneously and without thought often causes depression as the person realizes he acted foolishly and, therefore, thinks he must be worthless.

The Valley of See-Saws

One would think with his magnificent victory, Elijah would have been ready to take on the world. Rather, he provides an illustration that we live in a valley of see-saws, up one minute and down the next.

It would seem good to always be up, but that would be impossible and unrealistic. Even Jesus Christ, with Peter, James, and John, on the Mount of Transfiguration had to return to the valley of life with its difficulties and stresses (Luke 9:28-45).

Mountaintop experiences deplete our energy because of the high emotional level on which we operate. It is necessary to return to routine—to rest, evaluate, and learn from the experience. Following such a high, the low dips lower before settling at a normal level. Our great enemy Satan is aware that this is also a place of depressed emotions, a prime time for him to race to the attack.

Rather than finding a place of respite and strengthening, Elijah was thrust on to the battlefield again, with his store of ammunition depleted.

Elijah's high was literally on a mountain, with God's tremendous victory over Baal worship. This sort of high could come in many forms: attending a stimulating seminar or spiritual retreat; preaching a powerful sermon or teaching a Bible class; sharing Christ with a neighbor; or receiving an answer to prayer. We need to recognize the see-saw lowering us to the ground and even to expect it. However, by being on guard we can avoid defeat.

"Be of sober spirit, be on the alert. Your adversary, the devil, prowls about like a roaring lion, seeking someone to devour. But resist him, firm in your faith, knowing that the same experiences of suffering are being accomplished by your brethren who are in the world" (I Peter 5:8–9).

Faith in Jesus Christ is sufficient to thwart the attacks of Satan, in the valley as well as on the mountain. With additional time resting and relaxing, conscious of God's care and protecting power, we can recoup our strength and renew our souls.

A Physical Cause

A third reason for Elijah's depression, and coupled with the valley of see-saws cycle of life, was his fatigue and hunger. He was exhausted and famished! Already that day he had spent hours on Mount Carmel in conflict with the prophets of Baal. The emotional tension of the challenge, building his own altar, the slaughter of the prophets, and the twelve-mile run back to Jezreel completely drained his strength. Before he had time for a good night's sleep or even a quiet meal, Jezebel's message arrived and he ran again.

By the time he flopped under the juniper tree, Elijah had traveled from Jezreel to Beersheba in Judah. There he left his servant, continuing another day's journey, probably a total of about one hundred miles. He had reason to collapse!

A weary body, pushed beyond its normal

energy level, can produce tired, depressed emotions.

Circumstances Rather than God

Elijah was depressed because he did not see the circumstances correctly. Taking his eyes off Jehovah-God, sender of fire and rain, he focused instead on the furious, fuming, godless, violent Queen Jezebel. If he had stopped to think, he would have remembered that surely the God who protected him against the king, his servants, and the prophets of Baal on Mount Carmel could protect him from one vicious woman.

Besides, if she had wanted to take his life she would have sent an executioner, not a messenger. Jezebel was too clever to martyr Elijah just at the time when Israel seemingly was about to experience national revival of Jehovah worship. Perhaps she feared contention with his fire from heaven. Regardless, she gave him the opportunity to flee. Now he could be remembered as a coward rather than a courageous man of God. With Elijah and his God-given power removed she could systematically eliminate anyone else who dared to promote Jehovah worship.

Whenever we focus our attention on the difficult circumstances rather than on the God of the circumstances we open the gate for depression to enter.

Unrealistic Expectations

In I Kings 19:4 we read, "It is enough; now, O Lord, take my life, for I am not better than my fathers."

Elijah was saying, "God, I've had it! There is no longer any need for me to live. I am weak, no better able to cope than my fathers before me. My ministry is no more successful than theirs. I am disappointed that you have not fulfilled my expectations and allowed me to accomplish great things for you. I put everything I had into it and I am a failure!"

Frustrated goals are a major cause for depression. It seems that Elijah demanded perfection for himself. Because he failed to attain to that level of performance he blamed God for letting him down, ignoring God's accomplishments through him.

Isn't it amazing how soon Elijah forgot? Had there ever been a boy raised from the dead up until this time? Had ever a man prayed that the rain would cease and it ceased? Was there in all the land another cruse of oil and barrel of meal that continued to supply for a hungry family? Who before him had called down fire from heaven? Elijah was depressed because he concentrated on unrealistic expectations for himself rather than his achievements.

Improper Self-concept

I Kings 19:4 reveals another cause of Elijah's depression: he compared himself unfavorably with others "For I am not better than my fathers" (I Kings 19:4).

In his mind Elijah saw Abraham, knife stretched over his bound and only son. He was ready to obey God even to the death of his long-awaited promise. No doubt Elijah remembered Moses stretching his rod over the Red Sea. As the waters rolled back, the people crossed on dry ground. Or he thought of the young man David, fearlessly facing Goliath, while all the rest of the armies of Israel trembled in fear.

And then he whimpered, "And all I can do is run panic-stricken under a woman's threat."

If Elijah had compared his strong points with the strengths of Abraham, Moses, and David, rather than his failures, he would have recognized his own self-worth instead of suffering from a deficient self-esteem.

Self-imposed Isolation

His depression was intensified by his self-imposed isolation from others. He left his faithful servant in Beer-sheba and went on alone to the juniper tree. Desperately he needed to know that someone loved him and believed in him. Yet, characteristic of the depressed, he rejected this source of help for his own painful solitude.

TREATMENT FOR ELIJAH'S DEPRESSION

God's encounter with His depressed servant reveals divine treatment, slowly but systematically and persistently carried out to bring healing and restoration. First, He met his physical needs of rest and food. Second, He allowed Elijah to run to the end of his self-sufficiency. Third, He identified the basic cause for Elijah's depression. Then He gave opportunity for Elijah to express his emotions and He provided an antidote for negative thinking. Finally God gave him a job to do. He concluded the encounter with encouragement, after revealing the truth and exposing Elijah's faulty thinking. Elijah's treatment con-

cluded successfully with his cooperation, bringing healing to his depressed state.

Physical Needs Met

To this dejected and defeated prophet drifted
the delightful respite of sleep. While he slept, I
wonder if he dreamed. I wonder if he saw an
angel busy beside a juniper tree, building a fire,
baking a cake, fetching a cruse of water from the
freshly filled stream.

"Elijah, Elijah, come and eat." His shoulder
shook and he heard a voice. He rubbed his eyes,
stretched and yawned, realizing that it wasn't a
dream. Before him lay provisions for his needs.
Hungrily, he ate and drank and promptly fell
back to sleep. How long did he sleep? Long
enough to be refreshed for a great journey,
when the angel again wakened him with his
lunch ready (I Kings 19:5–7).

The tenderness and care with which God
treated his depressed child is almost overwhelming. He neither scolded him for his cowardice
nor sympathized. To scold or accuse would have
added guilt to his depression, causing him to
sink further. To sympathize with his plight by
saying; "Poor boy, I know you must really feel
terrible. And who wouldn't after what you have

gone through!" would have promoted self-pity. God merely met Elijah's needs.

When I am tired I become depressed easily. It may be following a late evening out. My first thought, "I talked too much. Oh, I wish I wouldn't always chatter so!" begins the downward spiral of negative thinking. Without any effort at all I can soon talk myself into a totally dark picture of life, and finally plop into bed depressed. Such depression directly relates to fatigue.

I have established a rule for myself. Tired? Don't talk! Being aware of the relationship between depression and fatigue in my life, I can keep it from happening or nip it in the bud by telling myself: "You're tired; you feel negative; you can make yourself depressed. Go to bed!"

Self-sufficiency Relinquished

Second, God allowed Elijah to run to the end of his self-sufficiency. After being refreshed one would have expected God to say, "Now, Elijah, back to your post!" How often do we attempt to play God in the life of another by saying, "Do this," or "Do that" when a depressed person, already dominated with faulty thinking is unable to cope with the pressure?

God had something else in mind for Elijah; a new glimpse of Himself. Understanding His prophet perfectly and with His purposes in mind, He planned for Elijah to continue this run to the end of himself.

In speaking of the believer being brought to the end of himself, Charles Solomon states in his book *Handbook to Happiness,* that "God first has to take him through a reduction process where he is reduced to nothing so that Christ might be everything—his all in all."[1] From human perspective we would say that Elijah had wasted his time. But from God's view, He accomplished this in Elijah's life—his reduction to nothing that He might be all.

With supernatural strength provided through supernatural food, Elijah traveled for forty days and forty nights to Horeb, the mountain of God (I Kings 19:8). A ten-day journey stretched from Beer-sheba to Mount Horeb. Elijah extended it into forty, wandering as he went, taking little side trips to investigate the valleys, to meditate by the springs. The depressed person aimlessly whiles away precious hours, filling days with useless activity, or staring emptily at drab scenery.

On Mount Horeb, Elijah hid in trepidation from his God. It was here that God had appeared in the bush to Moses (Exod. 3:1) and delivered the law with an awesome display of His presence (Exod. 19, 20). By this same mountain the sinning Israelites stripped themselves of their ornaments as they stood waiting for the judgment of God (Exod. 33). Here also, God approached His overwrought servant, emptying him of his self-confidence, his lack of trust, his discouragement, his self-pity. In God's timing and patient waiting, He led His despondent friend through wasted wandering and depression to His mountain, His place of correction and commandment.

Initial Cause Identified

Elijah set up housekeeping in a cave, with only the bats to dispel his solitude and loneliness. His depression and preoccupation with his problems led him out of the joy of a right relationship with God. But God didn't wait for Elijah to discover his own plight and return in repentance. He sought out His erring one, to bring him back to Himself.

A third step in dealing with Elijah's depression is that God identified the initial cause, Elijah's impulsive action. A penetrating question from God interrupted his reveries.

"What are you doing here, Elijah?" (I Kings 19:9). Elijah ignored the query, side-stepping the truth convicting him of his impulsiveness. He was where he did not belong, and God eventually brought him back to the truth by repeating his direct question.

"What are you doing here, Elijah?"

God is always specific in His conviction. The vague feeling of guilt and depression twirling through our minds like a color wheel is not from God. He puts His finger on the root of the problem and probes. But graciously He explores only one area at a time. If we were confronted all at once with our failures and sins, the areas of falling short of God's holy standard, we would be crushed.

Emotions Freely Expressed

Not demanding an answer to His first question, God patiently allowed Elijah to express his pent-up emotions without censure or criticism, an important step in helping lift a person's depression.

"I have been very zealous for the Lord, the God of hosts; for the sons of Israel have forsaken Thy covenant, torn down Thine altars and killed Thy prophets with the sword. And I alone am left; and they seek my life, to take it away" (I Kings 19:10).

Elijah's evaluation was incorrect, but God

didn't accuse him. He listened as Elijah spewed out his fears, frustrations, and feelings of intense aloneness.

Suppressed negative emotions hide like an infected, putrifying sore under a spotless bandage. As the bandage must be removed and the wound cleansed before healing occurs, so it is helpful to reveal feelings.

I am not offering a license to spit out the venom of negative thoughts and emotions, complaints and criticism. I do not condone whining self-pitying songs to any unsuspecting person who happens to be available. Throwing books across a room, jumping, and screaming are certainly not legitimate expressions of frustration and depression. But God does offer Himself as a sounding board for the expression of feelings and emotions. David, in the Psalms, provides a myriad of examples for expressing his heart's deepest needs to God, the negative as well as the positive.

"O Lord, do not rebuke me in Thine anger,
Nor chasten me in Thy wrath.
Be gracious to me, O Lord, for I am pining away;
Heal me, O Lord, for my bones are dismayed.
And my soul is greatly dismayed;
But Thou, O Lord—how long?
Return, O Lord, rescue my soul;

Save me because of Thy lovingkindness.
For there is no mention of Thee in death;
In Sheol who will give Thee thanks?
I am weary with my sighing;
Every night I make my bed swim,
I dissolve my couch with my tears.
My eye has wasted away with grief;
It has become old because of all my adversaries"
(Ps. 6:1–7).

The writer of Hebrews exhorts us to come boldly to the throne of grace to obtain mercy and find grace to help in time of need. Until we learn to go directly to God and find this help, sometimes we need an intermediary, a pastor, husband, friend, or counselor—someone who can listen and love at the same time.

I grew up unable to express emotion, especially anger or hatred. Because it was wrong, and I didn't want to be wrong, I denied the presence of such feeling which turned inward to deep depression. Years later it all erupted with volcanic force.

We need to express such feelings in confession, realizing God's forgiveness stands available through Jesus Christ. We need to forgive the one causing our anger as well. Anger dissipates with forgiveness—both received and given.

Antidote for Negative Thought Provided

God attempted to direct Elijah's thought pattern from negative introspection to a positive revelation of His Person.

"I have something for you to see."

Before Elijah's vacant stare, the hopeless expression of the depressed, God displayed His power. Raging wind split the mountains asunder and tore up rocks like bits of paper. An earthquake quivered and trembled under foot. Crevices gaped open, causing deafening landslides before Elijah's now astonished eyes. Tongues of flame flashed—leaping, dancing, destroying. But the Lord was not in the wind, the earthquake, or the fire.

In the solemn quiet that followed God spoke "with the sound of gentle stillness" (Hebrew). Elijah recognized its powerful source and, wrapping his mantle about his face, approached the mouth of the cave in humility.

The voice repeated the question with firmness, yet with gentleness. "What are you doing here, Elijah?"

Elijah still showed no repentance, only reiterated his previous bewailing (I Kings 19:4). In effect he said, "God, I've seen your power and I know I'm weak, but I still see things the same way. I still feel all alone."

Elijah was left with his negative thought pattern for a while, but the fantastic display of God's power was not wasted, as is seen by his readiness to obey God's new orders. The depressed person doesn't always snap out of it immediately. As positive thoughts force their way through the wall of despair, it weakens; and, with continued persistence it eventually gives way. Other times God takes depression away instantaneously as thoughts focus on His truth.

New Purpose and Direction Given

God did not debate with Elijah, nor try to convince him that he evaluated the circumstances incorrectly. God shows us another important factor in dealing with the depressed: He gave Elijah a job to do, which involved the lives of other people.

"And the Lord said to him, "Go, return on your way to the wilderness of Damascus, and when you have arrived, you shall anoint Hazael king over Syria; and Jehu the son of Nimshi you shall anoint king over Israel; and Elisha the son of Shaphat of Abel-meholah you shall anoint as prophet in your place" (I Kings 19:15,16).

With this command God caused Elijah to lift his eyes off himself and see the prospects of fruitful activity.

The command does not demonstrate that God considered Elijah a failure, but rather His commission to a new aspect of ministry. This is true for two reasons:

First of all, several years passed before Elijah was translated. In I Kings 20 we read of two Syrian campaigns against Israel, which involved two years at least. In chapter 21 Ahab sauntered through his stolen vineyard. Two or three years must have transpired since the drought to restore the fertility of the land. In 22:1 we read, "And three years passed without war between Syria and Israel." So a minimum of five years elapsed before Ahaziah became king in place of Ahab (I Kings 22:51), and reigned for two years. All during this time Elijah was training his successor, as well as other young prophets—at least fifty (II Kings 2:7).

Second, when God's servants in Scripture died as failures, they just died. Saul died a failure, a suicide, after God forsook him because of his sins of disobedience. In sharp contrast we read of Elijah translated in a chariot of fire, escorted by heavenly fiery horses into heaven. (II Kings 2:11). No, Elijah's depression did not cause him to live out his life as a failure. He victoriously finished his life because he obeyed God in his new ministry.

A bout with depression does not necessitate

sitting on God's shelf for the rest of our lives. It depends on our response to the depression. We can choose to learn from the encounter and emerge loving God more and understanding ourselves better, or we can spend the rest of our lives in self-pity. God offered Elijah a choice.

Faulty Thinking Exposed

As Elijah turned to obey with the strength imparted to him by God, the cloud of depression lifted; a glimmer of hope sprang up within his weary heart; a hint of purpose and determination flashed across his face.

"And by the way," said God, "you're not really alone. Besides you there are seven thousand others who have not bowed to Baal." Finally, He clarified Elijah's faulty thinking pattern by pointing out that he had misunderstood the entire picture.

Cooperative Response Brings Healing

First, Elijah revealed his feelings honestly to God. He didn't engage in following a list of rules for his own deliverance. A depressed person is often incapable of lifting himself out of his plight. He's too depressed! Elijah just openly expressed his emotions of worthlessness and despair. Free communication with God is essential to emotional healing. Too often Christians deny negative emotions, because they cannot admit the reality of sin in their lives. In suppressing or ignoring them, they merely cause problems in other ways: anger, psychosomatic symptoms, pride, or self-righteousness. Rather, we need to admit our human weaknesses to God, allowing Him the opportunity to reprogram our minds. "And do not be conformed to this world, but be transformed by the renewing of your mind, that you may prove what the will of God is, that which is good and acceptable and perfect" (Rom. 12:2).

Second, Elijah obeyed God's recommissioning. He could have ignored God's command and stayed in the cave holding a pity party with the bats. His first faltering step in the direction of obedience chased away his gloom.

"In everything give thanks: for this is the will of God in Christ Jesus concerning you" (I Thess. 5:18, KJV). This command rings contrary to the way we feel when things do not go our way. Obedience, even if it is a weak "Thank you, Lord, because I know you are trustworthy," will begin to chase away the fog of depression and allow a glimmer of sunshine to filter through.

In this encounter God tenderly and patiently sought out His depressed child. He gave Elijah the necessary time to get to the bottom, so the only place he could look was up. He identified the problem and then showed Elijah a fresh glimpse of Himself.

This is the key to the lifting of Elijah's heavy cloud: a fresh glimpse of the Lord! In looking at God, Elijah took his eyes off himself and his circumstances. Relief from depression resulted supernaturally and automatically. Then—and only then—Elijah heard the command of God to return to his ministry!

Elijah traveled to Damascus a stronger man because in his weakness he saw the power of God. In his aloneness God sought him. In his despair God gave him direction.

RESULT OF GOD'S TREATMENT

There are several positive results recorded in the life of Elijah following his encounter with depression and with God. First of all, Elijah experienced personal spiritual growth. In admitting his own inadequacy, the prophet more fully served with God's adequacy. He then enjoyed the privilege of training his successor, and of victoriously confronting his old enemy, Ahab. His faith demonstrated maturity in his contention with Ahaziah. His ministry multiplied through the school of the prophets, and finally God Himself extolled Elijah's life.

Personal Spiritual Growth

Having experienced God's tenderness and concern, Elijah's own thundering disposition would be tempered as he dealt with others who were weak and failing.

Some have judged Elijah for the fact that he ran, prohibiting Israel from ever achieving national revival. I wonder if we can say dogmatically that God planned national revival for Israel. Or can we say that one man's impulsive act thwarted the sovereign purposes of God?

Remember the sin of Jeroboam, the first king of Israel. He made golden calves to worship, anointed ordinary men as priests, and established new feast days to prevent his people from returning to worship at Jerusalem. I Kings 14:16 says, "And He will give up Israel on account of the sins of Jeroboam, which he committed and with which he made Israel to sin."

Certainly all the results of the Mount Carmel victory were not lost in the hearts of the people who had cried out, "The Lord, He is God; the Lord, He is God" (I Kings 18:39). God graciously used the circumstances resulting from Elijah's impulsive decision to enrich his life in a spiritual way that cannot be measured by numbers won or by outward happenings.

As mentioned earlier, Elijah needed to come to the end of himself that he might know God more intimately, relying only upon Him for strength and power to accomplish his ministry. "That the proof of your faith, being more precious than gold which is perishable, even though tested by fire, may be found to result in praise and glory and honor at the revelation of Jesus Christ" (I Peter 1:7).

Elijah's faith, tried in the fires of depression, resurged to bring glory and praise to God.

Successor Trained

As Elijah left the cave—his experience encapsulated in a corner of his mind—he returned to Israel to obey his God. He first chose Elisha to be his successor and carefully trained him for the prophetic office. One man building into another man's life to carry on a significant ministry—who can measure the value in God's sight? Throughout history God has dealt in special ways with individuals rather than with the masses (I Kings 19:9–21).

He chose Abraham out of the multitudes in Ur of the Chaldees; a special recipient of faith and demonstration to the world (Gen. 12–25).

Jesus Christ trained twelve ordinary men from among the masses to carry on His work. Of the twelve, three received special instruction: Peter, James, and John (Matt. 17:1–9; 26:37, 38).

Elijah had at least seven years, as discussed previously, to train Elisha in the prophet's ministry. Had he been a spiritual dropout because of his depression, he would not have qualified to train his successor.

Enemy Confronted

Elijah was also given another chance to confront Ahab for his sin and rebellion against God. He cried and whined for a vineyard, like a spoiled child, until Jezebel rescued him. She killed Naboth, the vineyard owner, so Ahab could claim the property. Fearlessly Elijah reprimanded Ahab and announced the dreadful details of his and Jezebel's death. Dogs would lick up his blood in the place of Naboth's execution. Dogs would eat Jezebel by the wall of Jezreel (I Kings 21:1–24)

Matured Faith Demonstrated

God's faithfulness was again proven as He protected Elijah from those who wanted to take his life. Ahab's son, Ahaziah, reigned over Israel following his death as predicted. It is said that "he did evil in the sight of the Lord and walked in the way of his father and in the way of his mother and in the way of Jeroboam the son of Nebat, who caused Israel to sin" (I Kings 22:52).

One day, by his upper window, Ahaziah fell out and was injured. As he lay in his bed he sent messengers to Baal-zebub, god of the fly, to enquire concerning his prognosis.

Elijah met the messengers on their way with a message from God. "'Is it because there is no God in Israel that you are going to inquire of Baal-zebub, the god of Ekron?' Now therefore thus says the Lord, 'You shall not come down from the bed where you have gone up, but you shall surely die'" (II Kings 1:3, 4).

Ahaziah retaliated by sending a captain with fifty men to take Elijah, who sat calmly on a hilltop. He had come to know God in such a way that he did not run in panic when the enemy came to get him as he had before.

Twice armor clanked and marching feet tromped up the hillside. Spears glinted and faces sneered as the king's men approached Elijah. Twice the ribald commander barked out his order. "O man of God, the king says, 'Come down'" (II Kings 1:9).

Twice a bolt of fire from God confirmed Elijah's calm response, "If I am a man of God" (II Kings 1:10, 12).

Elijah once more demonstrated his faith in God as his protector. The third captain with his fifty men approached the hill with dread and dismay. Prostrate in the dirt before Elijah they begged for mercy; and, because of their humility, God told Elijah to return with them to the king.

Ministry Multiplied

Little is said about the remaining years of Elijah's life but no doubt he maintained victory over depression with his involvement in the lives of other people. He taught Elisha the knowledge of the power and love of God. He also invested his time heavily in the school of the prophets, using every opportunity to establish young men in a solid trust and faith in the living God. He strengthened them in boldness and courage to withstand the onslaughts of idolatry and licentiousness of their day and trained them to take up the reins of spiritual leadership.

Fifty of these men timidly followed Elijah and Elisha, watching from a distance as the worn mantle of the tempestuous man of God struck the torrential Jordan River. The river obeyed the power behind the mantle, allowing the prophets to cross over on dry ground. But if the parting Jordan caused astonishment for the watching seminarians, how much more the wonderment of Elisha, as he felt the whirling wind and beheld the chariot and horses of fire catch his master away and disappear into the clouds (II Kings 2:1–12).

Was the visible splendor of Elijah's departure for Elisha's benefit alone? Was it not also for those of us who find ourselves under the juniper tree wishing to die?

God rescued Elijah from the whirlpool of depression that was threatening to engulf his very life. He resumed the demonstration of His power through His humbled servant and gloriously transported Elijah to His presence, allowing him to escape the trauma of death. Only one other in Scripture, Enoch, experienced this privilege.

Life Extolled

Other Scriptures dynamically reinforce the fact that Elijah was not rejected by God.

Malachi wrote, "Behold, I am going to send you Elijah the prophet before the coming of the great and terrible day of the Lord" (Mal. 4:5).

John the Baptist fulfilled this prophecy as recorded in Matthew 11:14. "And if you care to accept it, he himself is Elijah, who was to come."

Elijah shared the unique privilege with Moses only, of chatting with Jesus Christ at the time of His transfiguration (Matt. 17:3).

As the words "My God, My God, why hast thou forsaken Me?" agonized from the dying lips of the Son of God, those standing by remarked, "This man is calling for Elijah. But the rest of them said, "Let us see whether Elijah will come to save Him" (Matt. 27:46, 47, 49).

Elijah was known and respected for his power for centuries to follow. Even James and John desired to command fire from heaven to consume their enemies as Elijah had (Luke 9:54). Paul referred to Elijah as an illustration of the believing remnant of Israel (Rom. 11:2–5). And finally James gave us Elijah as an example to follow in effectual, fervent prayer (James 5:16–18).

Pulling the blankets snugly around my shoulders, I closed my weary eyes to blot out the late morning sun streaming through my bedroom window. My world was drab and useless—I was depressed! I tried to forget that the remains of breakfast still cluttered the table and it was nearly noon.

"What are you doing here, Vivian?" spoke the voice of quiet gentleness in my foggy mind. I remembered Elijah.

All my defensive thoughts and arguments with God were stilled by the shrill ring of the telephone. My neighbor had to rush to the doctor. Would I keep her little boy?

In a flash I was dressed and had the dishes

cleared. Suddenly I realized the depression had evaporated. God had given me a task to accomplish.

He wants to show us a fresh glimpse of His Person and His love for us. We must look to see His power demonstrated in our world, and His purposes for us. Then, like Elijah, we can follow Him out of the cave to a greater ministry in the lives of our families, neighbors, or business associates.

1. Charles R. Solomon, *Handbook to Happiness* (Wheaton: Tyndale, 1975), p. 110.

2

GRIEF REACTION
R X: Naomi

The Book of Judges contains a sad commentary of the history of God's chosen people as they were caught in a cycle of defeat, temporary victory, and defeat again. God commanded the people to completely destroy their enemies occupying the Promised Land. But an oft-repeated phrase of chapter one explains their failure. "But the sons of Benjamin did not drive out the Jebusites who lived in Jerusalem; . . . Neither did Ephraim drive out the Canaanites who were living in Gezer; . . . Zebulun did not drive out the inhabitants of Kitron" (Judg. 1:21, 29, 30). The refrain continues for all the tribes of Israel. Failure in complete obedience resulted in catastrophe and suffering.

Finally the angel of the Lord appeared with a frightening pronouncement. "I brought you up out of Egypt and led you into the land which I have sworn to your fathers; and I said, 'I will never break My covenant with you, and as for you, you shall make no covenant with the inhabitants of this land; you shall tear down their altars.' But you have not obeyed Me; what is this you have done? Therefore I also said, 'I will not drive them out before you; but they shall become as thorns in your sides, and their gods shall be a snare to you'" (Judg. 2:1–3).

Israel bowed before heathen idols and engaged in licentious living. Chains of subordination rattled and bound her to her enemies as the cycles of defeat to partial victory began. Brought low into slavery, she cried out to God, who then sent a judge-deliverer and freedom. Freedom resulted in lethargy, compromise, and recurrent idolatry. God then punished with enemy attack and defeat until she again cried out to God, who sent a judge once more to free her. Repeatedly, she forgot God and worshiped idols until the slave chains rattled again.

One brief explanation sums up the decadence of this historical period. "In those days there was no king in Israel; everyone did what was right in his own eyes" (Judg. 21:25).

Out of this turbulent scene stepped a man and his family. Down the dusty trails leading away from Bethlehem they trudged, wending their way through parched Judean hills. Elimelech led the way, guiding his only donkey laden down with possessions and scant remaining supplies.

Under shaggy brows, Elimelech's dark eyes gleamed with anticipation as he directed their way toward Moab, where he expected to find a better life.

Two young sons, Mahlon and Chilion, followed along, at times bantering in friendly manner, often engrossed in heated debate over the political and spiritual scene left behind. If Gideon were really such a great judge, why did God send the famine? Yet it was exciting to retell the dynamic account of Gideon's victory over the Midianites. Imagine them slaying one another in their panic, caused by a few men blowing trumpets and breaking pitchers! It must have been a ludicrous sight (Judg. 7).

Occasionally their father interrupted the unceasing conversation to remind them that the famine came as a warning from God to turn from idolatry and worship Him. Perhaps he warned them, too, of the gods of Moab they would soon encounter, the cruel Molech and goddess Ashteroth.

"If we forget Jehovah in this foreign land, my sons, we too will suffer."

Deep in her own thoughts, Naomi trailed behind, pausing to gaze longingly backward at familiar places. An unbidden tear trickled its way down her wrinkling cheek, a depressing sigh heaved her weary breast.

"Oh, that my people would obey the one true

God, then the dry, barren fields would flush with grain and refreshing streams would flow from fertile hills." A sob catching in her throat, she turned to overtake her family, a new determination in her step and set of purpose on her aging face.

Scripture bluntly describes their first tragedy. "Now they entered the land of Moab and remained there. Then Elimelech, Naomi's husband, died; and she was left with her two sons" (Ruth 1:2, 3).

Perhaps the long journey through a dying land under a scorching sun proved too much for old Elimelech; we are not told. But this loss must have tightened poor Naomi's heart, comforted only in small degree by her two sickly sons. Soon Mahlon and Chilion married Moabite girls, but true to the meaning of their names "sickly" and "wasting" the sons lived only about ten more years and died also.

Naomi, in her grief, plummeted to the depths of loneliness, subsequent depression, and bitterness toward God. Hearing that the famine in Bethlehem had ended, she decided to go home.

STATEMENT OF DEPRESSION

Two bedraggled figures at last reached the brow of the hill leading down to the village of Bethlehem nestled in the valley below.

"Look, two women approach, alone."

"Who could it be?"

"Why it isn't, it couldn't be Naomi!"

"But it is!"

The entire town stirred at their appearance. Women bustled about to prepare a welcome, but in her depressive state, Naomi rejected their glad greeting. "Do not call me Naomi; call me Mara, for the Almighty has dealt very bitterly with me. I went out full, but the Lord has brought me back empty. Why do you call me Naomi, since the Lord has witnessed against me and the Almighty has afflicted me?" (Ruth 1:20, 21).

CAUSES OF DEPRESSION

There were four causes for Naomi's depression. She experienced reactive depression due to grief over the loss of her family and also resulting from her sense of displacement. Misunderstanding of God's person and an inadequate sense of her own worth compounded her depression.

Reaction to Grief

The major cause for Naomi's depression was the tragic loss of her family. With two sons to care for her and provide comfort in her loneliness after the death of her husband, she no doubt found meaning to life. But now with both sons having died within a brief span of time, a heavy blanket of hopelessness and despair smothered Naomi, overcome with grief.

A sense of loss is the substance of reactive depression. The person feels that permanence is demolished and the patterns for survival and security are scattered to the winds. The loss, whether real or symbolic, looms so great to the person that he responds by mourning it inconsolably, certain that he can never fill the empty space that it has left. This mourning or grief is the reactive depression.[1]

A person suffering such a loss as Naomi's experiences excruciatingly painful grief. Her emotion of grief is not to be judged as sin, but as predicted and normal reaction to such loss, which needed time to be expressed and worked through.

Result of Displacement

A second factor in her depression was her sense of displacement. She was left not only without husband and sons, but in a foreign land, among strangers, worshipers of unfamiliar and useless gods. Evidenced from the fact that Ruth chose to worship Naomi's God, she had not deserted her faith or failed to worship as a devout Jewess. Naomi, no doubt, had never really felt at home in this strange land.

Paul Tournier put this in an excellent phrase, titling his book, *A Place for You.* Every person needs a "place" of security and belonging. Depression often follows a move to an unfamiliar location, until the emotional transition is made.

Having lived in five different cities since marriage, I understand that sense of displacement. I have felt that underlying constant low-grade depression in the midst of lovely surroundings until emotional ties with the past are severed and my "place" is realized.

In Jesus Christ is a "place." As long as security is sought from people, places, or positions, inner striving and restlessness haunts the life. Ephesians 2:4–6 tells us that because of God's great love, He has made us alive in Christ and raised us to be seated with Him in heavenly places.

My recent move to Colorado taught me this truth in a new way. Loneliness and disquiet followed me through busy days. Every time a letter arrived from a friend, I had another "cry-in." I longed for the "place" from which I had come.

"Vivian, God is your security. Snuggle up

next to Him, allowing Him to love you and meet those security needs."

The words were gentle, yet probing. I had been caught in the trap of looking to people and places to meet needs that only God could meet.

"I sought the Lord, and He answered me,
And delivered me from all my fears.
O taste and see that the Lord is good;
How blessed is the man who takes refuge in Him!" (Ps. 34:4, 8)

How satisfying it is to know refuge in such a loving Father!

Dr. Cammer speaks also of displacement as a cause for reactive depression.

> When someone is uprooted, for whatever reason, he or she discovers that it is more than a mere "get up and go." Harsh losses are involved. Friendships made over a period of years must be left behind—together, possibly, with a lovingly tended garden, a familiar view from windows or patio, and the intimate sounds and smells of a long-settled house. These orientations to time and place relax the person, but with displacement he loses these bonds. Unknowns lie in wait at every turn. Each particle of living must now be anticipated.[2]

Because Naomi's religious and racial differences kept her from being incorporated into the Moabite culture and community, she must have constantly endured the restless undercurrent of depression that plagues a person without a place.

Misunderstanding of God

The third cause adding to the depth of Naomi's depression was her failure to understand the true person and character of God, which she expressed in bitterness and despair. "No, my daughters; for it is harder for me than for you, for the hand of the Lord has gone forth against me (Ruth 1:13).

"And she said to them, 'Do not call me Naomi; call me Mara, for the Almighty has dealt very bitterly with me. I went out full, but the Lord has brought me back empty. Why do you call me Naomi, since the Lord has witnessed against me and the Almighty has afflicted me?' " (Ruth 1:20, 21).

Naomi lashed out against God, seeing Him as harsh, cruel, and withholding. The true concept of Jehovah-Jireh, "the God who provides," faded into obscurity by her grief and depression.

She expressed what so often is uttered when

individuals suffer grief or hardship: "Why did God do this to me?" A misunderstanding of God's character at such a time results in depression. God has not promised a life free from sorrow, suffering, and trials. He has promised to provide grace and strength for those trials.

Abraham learned the concept of Jehovah-Jireh when God asked him to sacrifice his only son Isaac. The battle waged in Abraham's emotions as he struggled to choose between his love for his son and his love for God. As Abraham surrendered his will to God, God did provide—a lamb in the thicket as a substitute for his son (Gen. 22).

Paul came to know the God who provides in II Corinthians 12:7–10. He pleaded with God to remove the thorn in his flesh; and God provided—not removing the thorn, but with promise of His sufficient grace and strength to endure the trial. Paul wrote, "And He has said to me, "My grace is sufficient for you, for power is perfected in weakness." Most gladly, therefore, I will rather boast about my weaknesses, that the power of Christ may dwell in me" (II Cor. 12:9).

God's promises to demonstrate love and provision through each difficult circumstance permeate the New Testament.

"And my God shall supply all your needs ac-

cording to His riches in glory in Christ Jesus"
(Phil. 4:19).

"And after you have suffered for a little, the
God of all grace, who called you to His eternal
glory in Christ, will Himself perfect, confirm,
strengthen and establish you" (I Peter 5:10).

The depressed person must cling to the
knowledge of the person of God when emotions
make him feel that God doesn't really exist.

Depreciation of Self

Associated with her wrong concept of God
was an incorrect evaluation of her own worth.
These two concepts are inseparable. Only as I
see God in His true character can I have a
proper self-concept.

Naomi poured out her sense of worthlessness.
"Return, my daughters. Why should you go with
me? Have I yet sons in my womb, that they may
be your husbands? Return, my daughters! Go,
for I am too old to have a husband. If I said I
have hope, if I should even have a husband to-
night and also bear sons, would you therefore
wait until they were grown? No, my daughters;
for it is harder for me than for you, for the hand
of the Lord has gone forth against me" (Ruth
1:11–13).

In this tearful and heart-rending scene, Naomi pictured a symptom common among the depressed—the desire to be alone. Even though at such a time the depressed person needs people who will be there and continue to love, she pushed them from her because of her own sense of worthlessness and despair.

TREATMENT FOR NAOMI

God's treatment for Naomi came subtly but surely to heal her wounded soul. He gave her direction for the present and gradual relief for her grief. He provided her needs, both physical and emotional, and gave her new purpose for her future.

Direction for Present

First of all, God directed the immediate decisions facing Naomi. Without a husband or grown sons to supply her needs, away from all relatives, how could a poor widow provide for herself? "Then she arose with her daughters-in-law that she might return from the land of Moab, for she had heard in the land of Moab that the Lord had visited His people in giving them food" (Ruth 1:6).

It was no mere coincidence that Naomi heard about the end of the famine. God had taken her husband and sons, leaving her behind for a purpose which He was about to accomplish. The starting place required her to return to Bethlehem.

Relief for Grief

God allowed Naomi to express her anger and frustration, a result of grief, and in expression the process of relief began. In *Don't Be Afraid to Die: The Christian Way of Death,* Gladys Hunt says:

> God understands about grief. The Son of Man is called "a man of sorrows and acquainted with grief." If we understand anything at all about the cross we know God understands suffering. Our grief, our confusion, our doubts, our anger are safe with Him. We can tell Him all of these—in sobs or in shouts—and He will hear us. We may have to wait to hear and see Him in return. We can't hear when we're screaming and we can't see properly when our eyes are blurred with tears. But He will wait. We determine our capacity to receive from God, but even here He uses time to heal our exhaustion and tenderness to heal our aches until we want Him.[3]

And so God waited for Naomi.

Provision for Needs

God proved Himself to be Jehovah-Jireh to Naomi. He met her needs through her daughter-in-law, Ruth. First, Ruth met her mother-in-law's emotional need of love, expressed with incomparable beauty in the familiar words: "Do not urge me to leave you or turn back from following you; for where you go, I will go, and where you lodge, I will lodge. Your people shall be my people, and your God, my God. Where you die, I will die, and there I will be buried. Thus may the Lord do to me, the worse, if anything but death parts you and me" (Ruth 1:16, 17).

When a person withdraws from his family and friends because of a depression that is often unrecognized and rarely understood, the tendency is to become exasperated and impatient. The sensitive depressive person receives this message as rejection and becomes further depressed.

The journey back to Bethlehem would have been unbearable for Naomi to travel alone. Every step reminded her of the years before when she had a strong, loving husband to lead the way and two sons who gave her pleasure. Every heart beat echoed the words, "They're gone. I'm alone. They're gone. God has forsaken me." Ruth steadfastly and comfortingly strode beside her, a proof of God's love.

The depressed person needs to be reminded of God's love, even though he does not feel it. Usually actions rather than words on the part of a loved one can be more readily understood. God has used my husband immeasurably to demonstrate love when I was too depressed to cope with life. At times he would tidy the house or play with the boys. He meant, "I love you. I'm sorry you are depressed."

However, the wisdom of God is necessary to understand the depression. Is she just feeling sorry for herself, using her negative emotions to bring sympathy? Or is she manipulating others for her own ends through depression? The person who is burdened with depression and not using it as an excuse for irresponsibility usually responds to hope and God's solution.

Through Ruth, Naomi's physical needs were also met. Young, strong, and energetic, Ruth willingly took the place of a peasant in the gleaning fields, gathering grain left by reapers to provide for the poor. She found herself, with God's leading, in the field of Boaz, a kind and godly man. Attracted to this striking Moabite girl, he commanded his workers to drop stalks for her on purpose. At the end of the day she had gathered a whole bushel of barley!

Naomi could not help herself! "May he be blessed of the Lord who has not withdrawn his kindness to the living and to the dead" (Ruth 2:20).

"Praise the Lord," Naomi cried excitedly. "Why that man is one of our closest relatives." Praise to God displaced her depression as the glorious morning sun dispels the chill of night. Naomi was on the road to the healing of her tortured soul.

Praise scatters depression. A song of praise to God lifts my thoughts from myself and my problems to God and His person. As I sing the words "Joyful, joyful we adore Thee, God of glory, Lord of love," while driving to the grocery store or picking up around the house, depression disappears.

Purpose for Future

The last step in God's treatment provided Naomi a purpose in life, seen in two steps. In her tired mind, clouded by depression, sparkled a thought. The sparkle grew to a shining light as her plan began to take shape.

"Then Naomi her mother-in-law said to her, 'My daughter, shall I not seek security for you, that it may be well with you?'" (Ruth 3:1).

With all the intrigue of a professional matchmaker Naomi outlined the plan to Ruth—an old Hebrew custom of the kinsman-redeemer. As her thoughts transferred from herself and her loss to a bright and happy future for Ruth, Naomi had no more time for depression. In chapters three and four, the beautiful love story of Ruth and Boaz unfolds, ending with the second step in giving Naomi purpose for life.

Ruth gave birth to a son, giving Naomi a major responsibility, that of his care. With this tiny new squirming life in her arms, Naomi experienced the words of Hosea. "Come, let us return to the Lord. For He has torn us, but He will heal us: He has wounded us, but He will bandage us" (Hos. 6:1).

Many people are depressed because they have little or no meaning to life—elderly widows living alone, retired men having been replaced at the job, teenagers disinterested in pursuing the materialistic lifestyle of their parents, and even parents who find their pursuits unfulfilling and sense a hollow ring to the meaning of their existence.

God has a plan for each life, and following it removes the depression caused by purposelessness. A lonely widow could bake cookies for the children down the street. The retired gentleman could mow the widow's lawn or devote time to the church, visiting or helping. The bored teenager could read to blind and elderly cast-aways in rest homes. The busy parents need to re-evaluate priorities, zeroing in on the needs of one another and of their children, giving God first priority. Involvement in the life of someone with needs chases away depression caused by meaningless living.

RESULTS OF NAOMI'S TREATMENT

There are four strategic results seen in God's encounter with this lonely widow. The first was praise rendered to God. Second, we are given a portrait of love in the midst of a perilous period of history. Third, Naomi was given the privilege of progeny, and fourth, we see a picture of Christ as the Kinsman-Redeemer.

Praise to God

Naomi's crippled, futile life was transformed into one of praise and usefulness. Through her pain, Naomi learned a new appreciation for the goodness of God. He doesn't take anything from our lives without a purpose, to replace it with something better—a deepening relation-ship with Himself. "For My thoughts are not your thoughts. Neither are your ways My ways," declares the Lord. "For as the heavens are higher than the earth, So are My ways higher than your ways, and My thoughts than your thoughts. . . . For you will go out with joy. And be led forth with peace" (Isa. 55:8, 9, 12).

Naomi could have lived and died in Moab, an unknown, pitiful, poor widow. Instead her life was offered as a sacrifice of praise to God. "Blessed is the Lord who has not left you without a redeemer today, and may His name become famous in Israel" (Ruth 4:14).

God desires our lives to be offered as sacrifices of praise. "Through Him then let us continually offer up a sacrifice of praise to God, that is, the fruit of lips that give thanks to His name. And do not neglect doing good and sharing; for with such sacrifices God is pleased" (Heb. 13:15, 16).

Turning to God in times of despair and allowing Him to work in our lives, however painful the process, results in a sacrifice of praise.

Portrait of Love

Naomi's story is recorded in God's inspired Book as a portrait of unselfish love—a beautiful example to follow in seeking to restore a depressed person to a place of usefulness and meaningful existence.

It paints a picture also of God's love for His lonely, displaced, grief-stricken child. He wants to meet our needs and, in His unlimited power and creative resources, He is able to do just that.

Privilege of Progeny

If Naomi had only known that she was to be the great-great grandmother of King David and ancestor of the Messiah Himself, her heart would have leaped with anticipation as she hurried back toward the city of Bethlehem. What an encouragement it is to turn to the One who can give purpose and direction for life in the midst of depressing circumstances.

Picture of Christ

Nowhere else in Scripture is recorded so graphically the meaning of the kinsman-redeemer law (Deut. 25:5–10). When poverty forced an Israelite owner to sell his property, the nearest relative was obligated to buy it back, that it might remain in the possession of the original family. Boaz became the kinsman-redeemer for Ruth and Naomi. He had the wealth to buy the property, the willingness to assume that role because of his love for Ruth, and he was a near-kinsman.

One of God's purposes in Naomi's life provided an illustration of the Kinsman-Redeemer seen in Jesus Christ. The wealthy Son of God, infinite and sinless, was the only One with the resources to redeem degenerate, fallen man out of the slave-market of sin. "Knowing that you were not redeemed with perishable things like silver or gold from your futile way of life inherited from your fore-fathers, but with precious blood, as of a lamb unblemished and spotless, the blood of Christ" (I Peter 1:18, 19).

Because of His unfathomable love He died the cruelest of deaths on a rude cross to complete that redemption. "Who gave Himself for us, that He might redeem us from every lawless deed and purify for Himself a people for His own possession, zealous for good deeds" (Titus 2:14).

Through the incarnation, God became man, that He might be related to humanity and, therefore, be qualified to die for our redemption. "Since then the children share in flesh and blood, He Himself likewise also partook of the same, that through death He might render powerless him who had the power of death, that is, the devil; and might deliver those who through fear of death were subject to slavery all their lives" (Heb. 2:14, 15).

As Naomi had to reveal her need of a

kinsman-redeemer to Boaz, each person sold into the bondage of sin must realize his need of One to redeem him. "And without faith it is impossible to please Him, for he who comes to God must believe that He is, and that He is a rewarder of those who seek Him" (Heb. 11:6).

Jesus Christ is our Redeemer, wealthy, willing, and qualified. "But as many as received Him, to them He gave the right to become children of God, even to those who believe in His name" (John 1:12).

Not only does Christ redeem us from sin, but also from slavery to depression's cruel shackles. "It was for freedom that Christ set us free; therefore keep standing firm and do not be subject again to a yoke of slavery" (Gal. 5:1).

---

1. Leonard Cammer, *Up From Depression* (New York: Simon and Schuster, 1969), p. 58.
2. Ibid., p. 62.
3. Gladys M. Hunt, *Don't Be Afraid to Die: The Christian Way of Death* (Grand Rapids: Zondervan, 1974), p. 6.

3

REJECTION SYNDROME
R X: Jeremiah

"Jeremiah," spoke the Lord to a timid, inse-cure youth living in Anathoth, "I knew you before you were born and have consecrated you to be my prophet to the nations."

"Oh no, Lord God. I cannot speak and am still too young," replied the trembling Jeremiah.

With God's encouragement, promise of pro-tection, and divine touch on his mouth, Jeremiah found himself unable to resist his commission to speak God's words (Jer. 1). In the thirteenth year of King Josiah's reign Jeremiah was on his way to becoming one of God's greatest prophets, yet speaking the most dismal message under the most adverse circumstances.

His message pronounced doom for Judah. God's judgment lurked at the door. Their idolatry and godless living caused His promise of captivity to pounce upon Judah as a screaming cougar attacks her unsuspecting prey (Jer. 6:11; 15:4, 6).

Manasseh seduced Israel to commit even more iniquity than all the Canaanite nations that God had destroyed because of their evil. Manasseh built altars for Baal, worshiped the hosts of heaven, and set their altars in the temple. He practiced witchcraft, divination, and dealings with mediums and spiritists. Innocent blood flowed from one end of Jerusalem to the other because of his cruelty.

God, provoked to wrath, sent a message through His prophets. "Behold, I am bringing such calamity on Jerusalem and Judah, that whoever hears of it, both ears shall tingle . . . and I will wipe Jerusalem as one wipes a dish, wiping it and turning it upside down. And I will abandon the remnant of My inheritance and deliver them into the hand of their enemies, and they shall become as plunder and spoil to all their enemies" (II Kings 21:12–14).

Revival under King Josiah was short-lived. With his wicked sons Jehoiakim, Jehoichin, and later Zedekiah, on the throne, Jeremiah suffered persecution and rejection.

All Judah lay in the squalor of idolatry, licentiousness, murder, and every kind of evil. She refused to heed Jeremiah's urgent pleas to repent in the face of pending disaster. He urged the Israelites to submit to Babylonian rule because it was from God, and thus, their lives would be spared. They accused him of treason and conspiracy with the enemy. (Jer. 21:8, 9; 27:1–13).

Jeremiah delivered God's message until the walls of the city crumbled under the attack of Nebuchadnezzar, king of Babylon. He helplessly watched as little children starved to death and ruthless soldiers ravaged defenseless women and dragged strong youths into slavery.

He couldn't even share relative peace with the poor remnant left behind to keep the vineyards of the Babylonian-occupied Judean hills. Rebel countrymen forced him to flee with them to Egypt. There he endured continual rejection of God's message, living out his life a homeless, lonely and rejected servant of God.

STATEMENT OF DEPRESSION

Because the Book of Jeremiah is not written in chronological order, it is impossible to relate specific historical facts to Jeremiah's times of depression. However, it is clear that he plummeted to the depths on more than one occasion, yet rose in victory to continue God's task. Jeremiah's temperament was such that he, no doubt, reacted with depression on many occasions. His sensitive nature and retiring manner increased the depth of his suffering. Tyrannical depression plagued him throughout his life, offering no escape from the pitiful environment in which he was forced to live.

Woe to me, my mother, that you have born me
As a man of strife and a man of contention to all
the land!
I have neither lent, nor have men lent money to
me,
Yet every one curses me (Jer. 15:10).
Cursed be the day when I was born;
Let the day not be blessed when my mother bore
me!
Cursed be the man who brought the news to my
father, saying,
"A baby boy has been born to you!"
And made him very happy.
But let that man be like the cities
Which the Lord overthrew without relenting,
And let him hear an outcry in the morning
And a shout of alarm at noon;
Because he did not kill me before birth.
So that my mother would have been my grave,
And her womb ever pregnant.
Why did I ever come forth from the womb
To look on trouble and sorrow.

So that my days have been spent in shame? (Jer. 20:14–18).

CAUSES OF JEREMIAH'S DEPRESSION

If there ever was a person who could claim justifiable cause for depression, it was Jeremiah. First, the rejection syndrome characterized his life. Then he could not escape the compulsion to preach a message of doom and destruction. Add to that his own physical suffering and the emotional weight of intense anguish of people around him. Finally, in his agony, he often lost sight of God's faithfulness.

Jeremiah's Rejection

Jeremiah's complete rejection was the basic cause for his depression. Even his family turned against him. "For even your brothers and the household of your father, Even they have dealt treacherously with you, Even they have cried aloud after you. Do not believe them, although they may say nice things to you" (Jer. 12:6).

Jeremiah was denied social acceptance. God forbade him to marry and have his own children (Jer. 16:2) because of the imminent disaster on the city. He wasn't allowed even to socialize with his countrymen, but was required, rather, to live a lonely and isolated life (Jer. 16:8).

For forty years Jeremiah trudged the alleys of Jerusalem with God's message to repent. He cried from the temple steps and preached in open courts. To the poor and ignorant, the great and mighty, he proclaimed God's truth, but not one heart repented. His ministry and his message were totally rejected (Jer. 5).

In his book, *The Ins and Outs of Rejection,* Dr. Charles Solomon says, "For the severely rejected, depression is a way of life."[1] Jeremiah's agony in relation to his rejection is poignantly expressed in Jeremiah 20:7, 8.

O Lord, Thou hast deceived me and I was deceived;
Thou hast overcome me and prevailed.
I have become a laughingstock all day long;
Everyone mocks me.
For each time I speak, I cry aloud;
I proclaim violence and destruction,
Because for me the word of the Lord has resulted
In reproach and derision all day long.

Because of the rejection Jeremiah suffered on a human level, he also felt rejected by God (Jer. 15:18; 20:7). Dr. Solomon bears this out. "The lack of acceptance on a human or psychological basis carries over into the spiritual realm. Not feeling accepted by others they do not feel accepted by God."[2]

Jeremiah followed the path of rejection by God to ultimate self-rejection, a desire to have never been born (Jer. 20).

Jeremiah's Divine Compulsion

There was no escape from the burning constraint within Jeremiah to obey God. Evidently he had tried to keep it in, to ignore God's hand in his life. But the strength of divine compulsion and urgency of the message burst out of his being as powerful waters break forth from a weak spot in the dam.

But if I say, "I will not remember Him
Or speak any more in His name,"
Then in my heart it becomes like a burning fire
Shut up in my bones; And I am weary of holding it in,
And I cannot endure it (Jer. 20:9).

In the following verses of this lament Jeremiah plunged to the depths of depression, wishing he had never been born. He knew pressure! Deep inward pressure from God at times threatened to blot out every bit of emotional strength he had.

Jeremiah's Personal Agony

Assaults on both body and emotions hounded Jeremiah's life. Everywhere his determined steps drove him, opposition mocked and derided. His life was constantly in danger as his enemies plotted for his life (11:18, 19; 18:23; 26:8; 36:26). Whipped by his enemies, he was thrust into the stocks in public disgrace. He endured arrest for crimes he didn't commit and spent long days in prison (20:2; 26; 37:14–16; 32:2; 33:1; 37).

As the Chaldean army surrounded the walls of Jerusalem, battering rams thudded against the ancient stones. Zedekiah, a weak and vacillating king, delivered the preaching Jeremiah over to his enemies. They tied him with ropes and lowered him into an empty, moldy cistern to starve to death. Sinking into the mire at the bottom, Jeremiah's emotions must have sunk too, as his old enemy depression slithered down the slimy walls to captivate his emotions once more (Jer. 38).

Jeremiah's Vicarious Suffering

Jeremiah no doubt witnessed as much or more agony in the lives of others than any other person recorded in the Bible. His sensitive soul grieved over idolatry and immorality rampant among the people. He suffered along with them in their physical distress. He listened as the sounds of war approached his beloved city—the clanking of armor, the stomping of horses, and the rumble of battering rams rolling over the hills.

My soul, my soul! I am in anguish!
Oh my heart!
My heart is pounding in me;
I cannot be silent,
Because you have heard, O my soul,
The sound of the trumpet,
The alarm of war (Jer. 4:19).

He heard the mocking cries of the priests and false prophets who rejected God's message and continued in their idolatrous practices.

As for the prophets:
My heart is broken within me,
All my bones tremble....
For the land is full of adulterers....
For both prophet and priest are polluted (Jer. 23:9–11).

Even the earth suffered under God's judgment. The ground cracked and lay barren under the scorching sun. Streams ran dry and cisterns emptied. Wild animals brayed in pathetic protest as their strength ebbed away and death stalked about (Jer. 14:1–6).

He witnessed slaves and lowly people beaten under the oppressive reign of ruthless and selfish King Jehoiakim (22). His heart grieved as the people followed the false prophets' messages of peace when there was no peace. They wandered like sheep following a wicked shepherd to their doom as he stood helpless to divert their path back to God.

As Nebuchadnezzar's army accelerated the attack and the city fell under seige, Jeremiah's suffering increased acutely. Starving mothers boiled their own babies and devoured them! Children died hungry and pitiful in the streets with no one to care. Priests groaned and fell under the sword in God's own sanctuary. Women and young girls endured cruel ravishing, and robust youths bore the yoke of slavery as they trudged over the desolate roads to Babylon. Destruction lay like a blanket of weeping over the fallen city. And Jeremiah's heart was broken.

My sorrow is beyond healing,
My heart is faint within me!
For the brokenness of the daughter of my people
I am broken;
I mourn, dismay has taken hold of me (Jer. 8:18, 21).

Jeremiah beheld the sin of God's chosen people and he bore the pain of God's punishment. Indescribable suffering of a city and its inhabitants—false priests and brave young men, innocent children and idolatrous women—filled him with hopelessness and despair—depression.

I watched the multitudes in our capital city go their ways in ordinary living; young women caught up in the confusion of false cults; teenagers seeking thrills in immorality, drugs, and drunkenness; businessmen and housewives worshiping gods of materialism and intellectualism. And even God's children cried "peace," oblivious to sin in their midst and to God's certain chastening. I have felt a small measure of Jeremiah's suffering for the plight of others and with it comes a sense of depression.

Jeremiah's Faltering Faith

"Wilt Thou indeed be to me like a deceptive stream with water that is unreliable?" (Jer. 15:18b). At times Jeremiah, overwhelmed with circumstances, lost his focus on the person of God. And well he might as daily God's pronouncement of judgment poured through his own lips. He spoke of death, the sword, famine, and captivity. He heard God say,

And I will winnow them with a winnowing fork
At the gates of the land;
I will bereave them of children, I will destroy
My people (Jer. 15:7).

He responded subjectively to the message and
forgot God's purpose for his life and His promise of protection. Whenever attention to circumstances dims the view of God's sufficiency, a
depressive-prone person becomes depressed.

TREATMENT FOR JEREMIAH'S DEPRESSION

Unlike the usual response of the depressed
person to run and hide from God or people as
seen in Elijah, Jeremiah is a beautiful example of
a deeply depressed individual beginning the
necessary treatment himself. He turned to the
Lord in his depression. Also he girded up his
mind to concentrate on the person, the charac-
teristics of God. God continued the treatment
by confronting Jeremiah with his wrong attitude.
He then met his needs through encouragement,
reassurance, and promise of protection.

Jeremiah Communicated the Problems to God

Why is it that so many people who are depressed grovel in their low emotional state alone?

Why do many flit from listening ear to listening ear hoping to find sympathy for their plight? Why do depressed persons take so long to turn to God?

Depression, an emotion, is merely a symptom of a deeper problem. The causes of the depression or hurtful results need confession. Depression may often erupt into anger, expressed by lashing out at a family member, or it may revert inward to self-pity. It may cause impulsive behavior of one sort or another. But the heavy cloud of depression, brought into the light of God's examination, results in healing. This is what Jeremiah did.

Jeremiah turned to God with confidence and strength when he was overwhelmed with self-debasement and despair. He must have previously made it his habit to look to God with all of his questions and deepest need.

Righteous art Thou, O Lord, that I would plead my case with Thee;
Indeed I would discuss matters of justice with Thee:
Why has the way of the wicked prospered?
Why are all those who deal in treachery at ease?
(Jer. 12:1).

Jeremiah discussed with God the age-old question of why the wicked seem to prosper while the righteous suffer. He also confided in God his confusion over the rejection of the chosen nation (Jer. 14:19–22). And when the men of Judah plotted against him to destroy him, Jeremiah pleaded his case before God (Jer. 18:18–23).

Therefore, in the time of Jeremiah's deepest need and lowest ebb, he automatically poured out his feelings of rejection, hopelessness, and despair-depression to the God who had been there in time of lesser need. Following his lament in Jeremiah 15:10, he cried out:

Thou who knowest, O Lord;
Remember me, take notice of me
And take vengeance for me on my persecutors.
Do not, in view of Thy patience, take me away;
Know that for Thy sake I endure reproach. (Jer. 15:15).

In chapter 20, Jeremiah again spewed out his feelings of rejection in pitiful mourning to the God who brings comfort and healing.

Jeremiah also had the habit of obedience which kept his line of communication open to God in times of crisis (12:1–7; 18:1–3). If we who respond to life stresses with depression would develop continuing communication with obedience on a daily basis, we would find we can also go to Him with depression and find relief.

I slumped down in the blue chair and stared aimlessly into space. An unbidden tear trickled down my expressionless face. What a pity that my world had to tolerate me, for I was useless and only a problem wherever I went. Oh that I had never been born to live out such an existence!

"When I get depressed, I turn to the Psalms and stay there," spoke a voice in my mind, a memory of a dear Bible Study Fellowship leader.

"Well, it won't do me any good," I responded.

Nevertheless, listlessly picking up my Bible, I opened to Psalm 139. I read it through once, then twice, then I began to memorize. By the time I reached verse 17,

How precious also are thy thoughts to me, O God!
How vast is the sum of them!

my depression had evaporated under the warming light of God's truth. He cares about me and has a purpose for my life!

Like Jeremiah, we need to develop the habit of taking our complaints to God, rather than scurrying around to find a listening and sympathetic human ear.

Jeremiah Concentrated on God's Character

The second thing that Jeremiah did for himself was to focus on the person of God. It is not because of our need only that God acts in our behalf, but because of His unfathomable nature as God. In the midst of Jeremiah's pathetic picture of affliction, suffering, abuse, and rejection in Lamentations 3, he catches a glimpse of the person of God.

The Lord's lovingkindnesses indeed never cease,
For His compassions never fail.
They are new every morning;
Great is Thy faithfulness (Lam. 3:22, 23).

Therefore he could say

For the Lord will not reject forever,
For if He causes grief,
Then He will have compassion
According to His abundant lovingkindness
(Lam. 3:31, 32).

The remedy for depression caused by rejection is acceptance. That seems simple enough.

But we cannot control our environment or force acceptance by others. A child, rejected by parents wittingly or unwittingly, by siblings or peers, grows up to feel rejected by God also. He feels that he is an unworthy person. "He can't really love me. No one else does."

The solution is found in the truth of God's Word and our acceptance in Jesus Christ. Paul says it beautifully. "Having predestinated us unto the adoption of children by Jesus Christ to himself, according to the good pleasure of his will, To the praise of the glory of his grace, wherein he hath made us accepted in the beloved" (Eph. 1:5, 6, KJV).

Jeremiah reminded himself of his acceptance by God in the midst of his depression.

Thy words were found and I ate them,
And Thy words became for me a joy and the delight of my heart;
For I have been called by Thy name,
O Lord God of hosts (Jer. 15:16).

What greater acceptance is there than to be called by the name of the Lord God!

What is the basis of our acceptance by God? It is through no merit of our own, but solely the work of Jesus Christ on the cross. "He made Him who knew no sin to be sin on our behalf, that we might become the righteousness of God in Him" (II Cor. 5:21). And again in I Cor. 1:30, "But by His doing you are in Christ Jesus, who became to us wisdom from God, and righteousness and sanctification, and redemption."

Having died and been raised with Christ, His righteousness, which is now my righteousness, meets God's requirements for my acceptance. He accepts me! "For you have died and your life is hidden with Christ in God" (Col. 3:3).

It is necessary for the depressed individual to focus his attention on his acceptance in Jesus Christ and on the character qualities of God. This renews the mind and raises the thoughts from shadowy introspection to a solid foundation of hope, trust, and freedom from depression.

Things were not going well in our new ministry. My husband was criticized and rejected at every turn. I stood by with encouragement and support, able to withstand the mud-slinging until one day it came my way.

"The reason your husband's ministry isn't successful is because of you. You need to become more involved."

"But I've been sick," I replied in self-defense.

"People don't seem to understand that because it has been so long. They feel they don't know you."

Later by myself the tears flowed; I wanted to

call somebody, anybody, to ask if it were true, but there was no one to turn to. If I could just cry on somebody's shoulder!

Sinking into the slime pits of depression, I caught hold of a saving rope in Psalm 26.

Vindicate me, O Lord, for I have walked in my integrity;
And I have trusted in the Lord without wavering.
Examine me, O Lord, and try me;
Test my mind and my heart.
For Thy lovingkindness is before my eyes,
And I have walked in Thy truth (Ps. 26:1–3).

I found Someone's shoulder to cry on, and discovered Him to be a trustworthy and righteous judge. He is filled with lovingkindness and is ultimate Truth. His wondrous works declare His power and because of His mercy I could plead my case with Him. I concluded with David that

My foot stands on a level place:
In the congregations I shall bless the Lord (Ps. 26:12).

If we gird up the loins of our minds by giving our attention to who God is in all His loveliness and perfection, negative emotions lose their ugly grip and scatter into hiding like unwelcome roaches when the light is switched on.

God Confronted Jeremiah with His Wrong Attitude

Why has my pain been perpetual
and my wound incurable,
refusing to be healed?
Wilt Thou indeed be to me like a deceptive stream
With water that is unreliable? (Jer. 15:18).

In his depression, Jeremiah lashed out against God. He saw God as an empty stream, unable to satisfy the thirst of a weary traveler. God dealt firmly with this wrong attitude.

Therefore, thus says the Lord,
"If you return, then I will restore you—
Before Me you will stand;
And if you extract the precious from the worthless,
You will become My spokesman.
They for their part may turn to you,
But as for you, you must not turn to them (Jer. 15:19).

It is important when dealing with the depressed to pin-point the basic problem. He often talks in circles, skirting the real problem, analyzing, comparing, and introspecting. Satan throws multitudes of fiery darts, causing confusion and guilt. But God is specific in his confrontation, and deals with one issue at a time.

Here God put His finger on the problem of Jeremiah's faulty thinking. He had allowed his emotions to control him rather than remembering God's truth and purpose for his life.

Emotions fluctuate as unpredictably as the song of a mockingbird. They rise or fall with the whim of the hour. I am increasingly impressed with the importance of the mind when God deals with His depressed children. He offers no panacea for emotional pain, no uppers or downers, not even sympathy. It is as though He ignores the emotional state and works directly with the root of the problem in the mind. We must choose to believe and obey the truth fed by God into the mind.

Today's culture is "feeling" oriented. We tend to put priority emphasis on how we feel. But God speaks to the mind. If we think properly, positive emotions eventually will follow. For some it may take a long time for those strong, negative feelings to change. With practice at turning our thoughts Godward, based on truth rather than on fickle emotions, depression's grip is weakened finally to the point of paralysis.

"Finally, brethren, whatever is true, whatever is honorable, whatever is right, whatever is pure, whatever is lovely, whatever is of good repute, if there is any excellence and if anything worthy of praise, let your mind dwell on these things" (Phil. 4:8).

God Promised Protection from His Enemies

"Then I will make you to this people
A fortified wall of bronze;
And though they fight against you,
They will not prevail over you,
For I am with you to save you
And deliver you," declares the Lord.
"So I will deliver you from the hand of the wicked,
And I will redeem you from the grasp of the violent." (Jer. 15:20, 21).

God encouraged his defeated prophet with His reassurance and promise of protection. Because Jeremiah had already learned that God was trustworthy, this declaration surely lifted his weight and sent him confidently back to his preaching. And God kept His word.

As Jeremiah languished in the mire at the bottom of his prison-well, he must have remembered this promise. And God delivered him (Jer. 38).

As Nebuchadnezzar devastated Jerusalem, leading a blinded and humiliated King Zedekiah into captivity, he set Jeremiah free. "Now Nebuchadnezzar king of Babylon gave orders about Jeremiah through Nebuzaradan the captian of the bodyguard, saying, "Take him and look after him, and do nothing harmful to him; but rather deal with him just as he tells you'" (Jer. 39:11, 12). God controlled the actions of godless men in behalf of his special servant, faithful to His promise.

Because of the unchangeable nature of God, the depressed one can find comfort in the eternal promises of God. "'For I know the plans that I have for you,' declares the Lord, 'plans for welfare and not for calamity to give you a future and a hope'" (Jer. 29:11).

God does not always give us immediate victory. Sometimes He has lessons for us to learn that can only be learned in the Valley of Weeping. Jeremiah lived his entire life in that valley, with only his faith in the character of God to provide hope for him, a hope that was never realized during his lifetime on this earth. But in that valley he came to know God. Our hearts cry out to know God. But do we accept the suffering that comes with it?

As a young teenager I cried out to God to show me His reality. In Jeremiah 29:13 He answered my cry. "And ye shall seek me, and find me, when ye shall search for me with all your heart" (KJV). My search led down many winding paths; some joyful and smooth but more frequently, rocky and painful.

I followed some of those paths through the Valley of Weeping, as depression, my constant companion, smothered me like an oppressive blanket. Often it seemed that there was no way out. But God had a purpose—to conform me to the image of Christ.

The refiner of gold builds a fire under his pot of metal. As bellows blow, the fire rages hotter and hotter, until the scum of impurity rises to the top. He cleans it off, layer after layer, gradually increasing the heat until he can see his own reflection in the shining liquid. Then the fire has accomplished its purpose.

Peter picks up this thought: "that the proof of your faith, being more precious than gold which is perishable, even though tested by fire, may be found to result in praise and glory and honor at the revelation of Jesus Christ" (I Peter 1:7).

Sometimes the fires are the circumstances

causing depression, and relief comes only when Jesus Christ can see His image reflected in us.

RESULTS

Jeremiah's experience with depression and its treatment shows three results. First, there was personal victory for Jeremiah in the midst of mind-breaking circumstances. Second, he won public recognition from God for his life and work. Third, he is a perpetual example that a life of praise can be lived in spite of insurmountable odds.

Jeremiah's Personal Victory

Even though Jeremiah's environment never became conducive to peaceful living, he found joy and comfort in his relationship to God.

Thy words were found and I ate them,
And Thy words became for me a joy and the delight of my heart (Jer. 15:16a).

As he evaluated the pitiful devastation of fallen Jerusalem, only Jeremiah's confident trust in God based on past emotional victories sustained him.

My eyes run down with streams of water
Because of the destruction of the daughter of
my people.
My eyes pour down unceasingly,
Without stopping, Until the Lord looks down
And sees from heaven (Lam. 3:48–50).

Jeremiah's Public Recognition

If you return, then I will restore you—
Before Me you will stand (Jer. 15:19a).

Jeremiah did repent and return to his task as
God's spokesman, and received God's recognition down through the centuries. His words
have been recorded with God's approval and included with the books of inspired writing. He
enjoyed the privilege of foretelling the coming of
the Messiah and joined the ranks of God's truly
great prophets (Jer. 23:5, 6; Matt. 16:14). Besides this, his name hangs in God's hall of fame
among the prophets, having gained His approval
through faith (Heb. 11:32–39).

Jeremiah's Perpetual Example

Surely no other person has endured such rejection and sorrow as did Jeremiah, the depressed, weeping prophet. If he could turn to

God with his complaints, so can we. Even as we find ourselves submerging under the ruthless waves of depression, we must raise our voice to God who hears every cry and understands each emotion. Thinking on God's person and powerful works transfers our thoughts from negative introspection, rescuing us out of the depths of despair. "As an example, brethren, of suffering and patience, take the prophets who spoke in the name of the Lord." Behold, we count those blessed who endured (James 5:10, 11a).

---

1. Charles R. Solomon, *The Ins and Outs of Rejection* (Denver: Heritage House), p. 44.
2. Ibid., p. 29.

4

SATANIC OPPRESSION

Rx: Job

Laughter, singing, and dancing permeated the elegant homes of Job's sons and daughters as they feasted and drank in merry celebration. Faithfully, Job arose each morning to offer sacrifices for them in case of sin, and God was pleased with Job.

"Have you noticed my servant Job?" God inquired of Satan who presented himself along with the angels of God in the courts of heaven. "See how honest and holy he is. He turns always away from evil, and honors and serves me above all else."

"Why shouldn't he?" scoffed Satan. "You've put a fence around him that even I can't penetrate. Take away his wealth, family, and protection, then listen to him curse in your face."

"Then the Lord said to Satan, Behold, all that he has is in your power, only do not put forth your hand on him" (Job. 1:12).

With insidious glee the evil one slithered out of God's presence to his work of terrorism.

"Now it happened on the day when his sons and his daughters were eating and drinking wine in their oldest brother's house" (Job. 1:13).

"Job, Job," panted the breathless messenger. "The Sabeans have stolen your plowing oxen and the asses and killed all the servants. I barely escaped to tell you."

Before Job could shake his head in disbelief, the door burst open again.

"Oh my master, great fire has fallen from the sky and burned up your sheep and servants. They lie in ashes and I'm the only one who is left to tell you."

Job's mouth dropped open in astonishment but with no time to answer as a third servant dashed into the room. "The Chaldeans, the Chaldeans!" They slashed all your servants with swords and drove away the camels. I narrowly escaped to tell you."

Immediately yet another servant barged in with the most painful news of all. "Master, master, your sons and daughters! While they were having a party a tornado blew suddenly from the wilderness and smashed down their house. Everyone is dead!"

Stricken with grief, Job tore his robe, shaved his head, and fell on his face to the ground and worshiped.

Naked I came from my mother's womb,
And naked I shall return there.
The Lord gave and the Lord has taken away.
Blessed be the name of the Lord (Job 1:21).

Triumphantly Job passed his first test under satanic oppression.

Again the angels came to present themselves before the Lord, Satan among them.

"Remember Job?" reminded God. "He is the most righteous man in all the earth, who held fast to his faith in me even though I let you ravage him without reason."

"Skin for skin," replied Satan. "A man will give up anything to save his life. Touch his own body and he will curse you to your face."

"He is in your hand," answered God. "But you must spare his life."

Satan departed to implement his diabolical scheme, inflicting Job with painful boils from the top of his head to the soles of his feet. Weighed down with pain and sorrow, Job sat among the ashes to scrape his draining sores with a piece of broken pottery. He longed for a word of comfort or hope, but the painful stillness was broken only by the sharp voice of his wife.

"Do you still retain your integrity? Curse God, and die."

"Don't be foolish" answered Job. "Do we expect only good from God and not evil?" "In all this Job did not sin with his lips" (Job 2:10).

STATEMENT OF DEPRESSION

The events of Job 1 and 2 transpired with such cataclysmic and rapid sequence it leaves one terrorized and breathless. It left Job sitting in forlorn destitution on his heap of ashes, surrounded by three friends who came to mourn his deplorable plight. For seven days and seven nights they sat in silence, so great was Job's grief.

"Afterward Job opened his mouth and cursed the day of his birth" (Job 3:1). Notice that Scripture didn't say "he cursed God," but "his day."

Let the day perish on which I was to be born,
And the night which said, 'A boy is conceived.'
May that day be darkness;
Let not God above care for it,
Nor light shine on it (Job 3:3,4).
Why did I not die at birth,
Come forth from the womb and expire?
Why did the knees receive me,
And why the breasts, that I should suck?
For now I would have lain down and been quiet;

I would have slept then,
I would have been at rest (Job 3:11–13).
Why is light given to him who suffers,
And life to the bitter of soul;
Who long for death, but there is none,
And dig for it more than for hidden treasures;
Who rejoice greatly,
They exult when they find the grave?
Why is light given to a man whose way is hidden,
And whom God has hedged in? (Job 3:20–23).

In essence Job reiterated, "Why was I conceived? But since I was, why couldn't I have been still-born or have died at birth? And since I didn't die then, why must I go on living now, a life of hopelessness and despair?" This was the agonizing heart-cry of a deeply depressed person.

CAUSES OF JOB'S DEPRESSION

The first cause of Job's depression was satanic oppression and harassment. Second, there was the intense pain of his physical condition, and third, a grief reaction due to the loss of his family and possessions. Last, he endured rejection by his wife and all of his friends.

Satanic Oppression

This torturous emotional and spiritual weight of direct satanic oppression threatened to crush the last bit of Job's faith. John 10:10 says, "The thief comes only to steal, and kill, and destroy." Satan came to Job, stole his possessions, killed his children, and destroyed his health, stopping only short of death. His affliction intensified the pain of all the factors compiled to create for Job a pitiful existence.

Satan not only attacks overtly as he did against Job's possessions, family, and body, but he attacks indirectly through our minds. This is how he approached Eve in the Garden.

"Indeed, has God said, 'You shall not eat from any tree of the garden'?" (Gen. 3:1).

He gained entrance into her thoughts as she listened and her resistance was lowered by the time the fatal fiery dart burned its way into her mind.

"You surely shall not die! For God knows that in the day you eat from it your eyes will be opened, and you will be like God, knowing good and evil" (Gen. 3:4, 5).

The result of Eve's allowing Satan to control her mind, of course, was devastating sin.

He produces depression the same way, throwing fiery darts of thoughts across the mind. An unalert believer claims the thoughts as his own, resulting in negative emotions and ultimate depression.

The enemy then moves in like a flood to oppress and harass, with ultimate intent to destroy. He whispers "peace" through withdrawal from reality or suicide. At times the false peace he offers sounds good to the depressed person looking for a way out of the horrible darkness of despair.

Physical Illness

The second factor to discuss in Job's depression is his physical condition. Boils infected every part of his body, from the bottom of his feet to the top of his head. Picture Job, the flesh of a strong man ravaged with draining, purulent sores. He could only attempt to relieve the intolerable itching with a piece of broken pottery. Each scratch caused reinfection until pain permeated his body. His eyelids, swollen and puffy, almost hid the glazed expression of his eyes, dulled by excruciating pain and inability to sleep restfully (Job 7:3, 4).

Leonard Cammer in *Up From Depression*, points out that "When generalized infection invades the body, through a virus for example, it can create toxicity to the brain and nervous system, and the person may be left with a depression which can last from one to two months."[1]

Depression may also come as a result of endocrine disorders, allergies, or following the trauma of surgery or other prolonged illness.

I found myself becoming increasingly depressed and unable to cope with any stress or confusion. Tears seemed to be always just a blink of pressure away and mere living became a trial. Accustomed to struggling with depression, I assumed it stemmed from emotional maladjustment as we had recently moved to a new city and a new ministry. I resumed the old habit of introspection to find the source of the problem, ignoring other factors like breathlessness at the top of the stairs and a positively grey complexion!

Finally, one day after a twenty-eight-mile bike hike, swimming, and softball with my high school girls' Sunday school class, I collapsed. Dragging myself into the doctor's office for a routine check, I surprisingly discovered my hemoglobin (iron content in the blood) was 6.4 (normal 12–15). I had reason to collapse! Subsequent treatment for anemia relieved not only the breathlessness and grey complexion, but also the depression. I could have confessed my depression as sin until I was blue in the face, instead of grey, and it would have accomplished nothing more than the promise of eventual collapse.

Medical and biochemistry studies have indicated many physical problems causing depression: chemical imbalance, nutritional insufficiency, hypoglycemia, and neurological defects.

Our fifth-grader began coming home from school unhappy. Life loomed bleak and unbearable. Classes were boring, piano lessons a drag, every small task an insurmountable chore. Apathetic, listless, and always close to tears, I often cried along with him.

"If I were talking about an adult, I'd say he was depressed," I explained to his teacher. Hanging up the phone, I realized, "He *is* depressed!"

My husband began spending extra time with him, talking, encouraging, working on a model. I sought to help with his chores to relieve some pressure. Nothing helped.

Finally one day his teacher asked, "How severe is Kevin's hypoglycemia?"

"I'm very careful. No sweets at all," I replied, "only on rare occasions."

"Well, the child next to him shares cookies and candy bars for lunch on a regular basis."

Keven had been treated with a proper hypoglycemic diet for about a year and a half, with good results. Not realizing the enemy, sugar, was back in the picture, we looked elsewhere for a cause for his depression. After only a few days of returning to his diet, the happy, creative child who loves life bounded in the house after school, eager to work on a project again.

A thorough physical examination and nutritional evaluation is essential to rule out a physical cause before treating depression on an emotional or spiritual level.

Grief Reaction

Reactive depression, as discussed in Chapter 2, is a normal response to the loss of a loved one in death or divorce, or in loss of possessions. Repressed anger or grief during this time results in depression of long duration and greater severity. Job suffered a grief reaction to both the material loss of his possessions and to the untimely death of his sons and daughters. He initially responded with worship and praise to God, but when the shock subsided, depression followed. The agony of his present circumstances stood out in striking contrast to his former days of prosperity and honor and the pleasure of his relationship to God (Job 29).

Rejection Syndrome

Job faced intense loneliness as a result of the rejection of his wife and friends (c. 19). As Eve was deceived in the Garden of Eden by Satan and then used by him to tempt her husband, so also Satan used Job's wife. More than any other time, Job needed the support and comfort of someone close to him, but it was not forthcoming. Instead, her words, expressing Satan's own heinous intent, rankled his tortured mind.

Some months may have elapsed between the time when Job's body was stricken and the arrival of his three friends, Eliphaz, Bildad, and Zophar (Job 7:3). They found him in a deplorable plight, maggots crawling through ulcerative eruptions, his skin black and peeling with rampant gangrene, his bones burning with fever—a living death. So great was their astonishment at his condition that they sat for seven days and seven nights without speaking.

Better was their comfort in silence than the barrage of words and accusations subsequently hurled at Job's tormented mind and withering body. Unknown to them, they joined hands with Satan in their attempt to prove Job a hypocrite.

"You've sinned, Job. That's why you're suffering. Confess, make it right, and your pain will cease."

Job was not only verbally rejected by his wife and friends but everyone else left him alone, returning only after his restoration. "Then all his brothers, and all his sisters, and all who had known him before, came to him, and they ate bread with him in his house; and they consoled him and comforted him for all the evil that the Lord had brought on him" (Job 42:11). Where were they in his hour of need?

SYMPTOMS OF DEPRESSION IN JOB

There are some interesting observations concerning Job in his depressed state which will be helpful in understanding the personality and responses of the depressed.

Introspection

A depressed person with an analytic mind can spend countless hours looking inward, examining his emotional and mental status. Job analyzed his situation and God's dealings with him to such a degree that he became confused about God's purposes (c. 9). He searched so diligently for the answer to "why" that he lost sight of the way of strength and support that only God could give.

When I am depressed, the automatic cycle of

introspection and subjective reasoning begins, offering no way out but only sucking me deeper into the mire of despair.

Self-defense

Not seeing God correctly, Job trapped himself in the snare of self-defense. The more his so-called friends accused him, the more adamantly he declared his innocence. However, someone must be to blame for his troubles, and since he was innocent, it must be God. A depressed person, having lost sight of God's goodness and care, often strikes out against Him. Remember, we viewed the panorama of chapters one and two, hidden from the eyes of suffering Job.

It is very difficult for depressive individuals to acknowledge their sin. Often perfectionistic by nature, they cannot accept the gross imperfections they see in themselves. Thus they loudly lament their innocence, hoping to still the inner accusatory voice of their own hearts.

Withdrawal

Job cried out to be left alone.

Withdraw from me that I may have a little cheer
Before I go—and I shall not return—

To the land of darkness and deep shadow (Job 10:20, 21).

To be left alone, although not helpful usually, is the longing of the depressed one. He feels that he is only a burden to everyone and unworthy of attention.

Abrupt Mood Changes

Job dramatically characterized wide mood swings, typical of the depressed. At one moment waxing eloquent in theological debate, his emotions rose to heights of sarcasm, great thought, and intellectual argument. The next he fell to the depths of his misery. Abrupt changes in mood can even intensify the depression. Often in an elevated emotional state, the person will act impulsively, later regret it, and sink even lower into depression.

TREATMENT OF JOB'S DEPRESSION

Job was treated from three sources. His friends tried to help him, unsuccessfully. He attempted to help himself through his own efforts to understand and communicate with God. First, he expressed his true feelings. Second, he intermittently poured out his heart to God. Third, he clung desperately to his belief in God; and last, he remembered former days of blessing.

Finally God stepped in to bring the treatment Job needed and with it healing. He first listened to Job. Second, He sent Elihu as his forerunner. Third, He appeared to speak directly to Job, captivating the attention of his mind. Last, He presented a true picture of His power contrasted with Job's weakness.

Friends' Inadequate Treatment

The treatment offered by Eliphaz, Bildad, and Zophar offers a striking parallel to many Christians today. When someone suffers, whether from financial disaster, loss of health, family death, or failure, they arrive first at the scene to offer senseless advice. Those who have never known the crushing weight of deep depression are the first to supply pat answers to pull the sufferer quickly from his plight. To those who follow the steps of the friends with their lack of understanding and open judgment I would say with Job, "Sorry comforters are you all. Is there no limit to windy words?" (Job 16:2, 3).

I sat in a discussion at camp, answering the question, "Is depression sin for the Christian?"

The answers came coldly and without sensitivity from those who obviously were never burdened with the problem.

"Because it can't co-exist with the fruit of the spirit which is joy, it must be sin and needs to be confessed."

"There is no reason for Christians to be depressed. It's wrong."

I noticed a sad-faced woman slip away from the group and hurry to her cabin. In a few minutes I followed, being quite sure she was hurt by the thoughtless discussion. I found her in tears as she poured out a story of a rebellious child and her inability to climb out of the depressive state she was in as a result of his behavior.

Instead of finding loving, caring, praying friends for her hour of need, the discussion had revealed a judgmental and unkind reaction to her already broken heart. She was not the object of the discussion, of course. Those who were insensitive to the hurt of depression were also unaware that she was in great emotional pain as she sat in the group.

Because I have traveled the road of depression with the inability to pull myself out of it, I am sensitive to this attitude which is prevalent among groups of believers everywhere. It leaves one more depressed, rejected, and guilty, compounding the problem.

How much more helpful it is to say, "I'm sorry you're hurting. I know how you feel, for I've been there. But I also know that in Jesus Christ there is freedom. May I share Him with you?"

"Blessed be the God and Father of our Lord Jesus Christ, the Father of mercies and God of all comfort; who comforts us in all our affliction so that we may be able to comfort those who are in any affliction with the comfort with which we ourselves are comforted by God" (II Cor. 1:3, 4). This applies to depression, also.

Job's friends offered him theological debate based on their own inadequate concept of God. He needed a fresh glimpse of the true character of God. They offered judgment and harshness. He needed encouragement and understanding.

For the despairing man there should be kindness from his friend;
Lest he forsake the fear of the Almighty.
My brothers have acted deceitfully like a wadi [a brook],
Like the torrents of wadis which vanish,
Which are turbid because of ice,
And into which the snow melts.
When they become waterless, they are silent,
When it is hot, they vanish from their place.
The paths of their course wind along,

They go up into nothing and perish (Job 6:14–18).

Attempted Self-treatment

Because of the nature of depression, it is very difficult for a person to help himself. Therefore, it is with great appreciation for Job that I see how he struggled for God and truth in the midst of his physical suffering and intellectual fog.

First, he expressed his true feelings. This was important. To deny emotions, even unhealthy ones, is to suppress them in such a way as to cause them to pop out unsuspectedly in a myriad of ways—psychosomatic symptoms, ulcers, coronaries, hostility, anxiety. I'm not justifying the fact of any child of God indulging in self-pity for weeks, months, or years. God's intent is that we should be joyful, offering daily our sacrifice of praise. I am saying that since depression does come because of our failures and weaknesses, we need to face it realistically. Sharing feelings honestly with God results in relief.

Job's mistake was that he talked to the wrong people. He recognized that he spoke impulsively and irrationally.

Oh that my vexation were actually weighed,
And laid in the balances together with my iniquity!
For then it would be heavier than the sand of the seas,
Therefore my words have been rash (Job 6:2, 3).

There are few people to whom you can reveal your hurting heart without receiving a judgmental or pat-answer response.

Second, he poured out his heart to God. Throughout his cycle of debate, Job moved from the defense of his innocence to a cry for God to hear him. This resulted in a growing trust in God, regardless of the outcome.

But I would speak to the Almighty,
And I desire to argue with God (Job 13:3).
O earth, do not cover my blood,
And let there be no place for my cry.
Even now, behold, my witness is in heaven,
And my advocate is on high. My friends are my scoffers;
My eye weeps to God (Job 16:18–20).

Depression is good suffering when it drives us closer to God.

Third, he hung desperately on to God. In spite of

his confusion and distorted thinking concerning God's character, Job clung to his immature faith in God. "Though He slay me, I will hope in Him" (Job 13:15). With these words a golden thread of faith began weaving its triumphant pattern through the dark, despairing tapestry of Job's plight.

When debating with his friends he defended his righteousness, justly. Job suffered not because of his sin, but because of his righteousness! (Job 1, 2) When he turned to God at intervals he indicated an understanding of himself as a sinner in the presence of a holy God (Job 13:23; 14:6). His faith exploded with an exultant cry of hope in 19:25–27.

And as for me, I know that my Redeemer lives, And at the last He will take His stand on the earth.
Even after my skin is flayed, yet without my flesh I shall see God;
Whom I myself shall behold,
And whom my eyes shall see and not another.

His broken spirit prevented him from maintaining this victorious level, until in his agony he cried out again.

Even today my complaint is rebellion;
His hand is heavy despite my groaning.
Oh that I knew where I might find Him,
That I might come to His seat! (Job 23:2, 3).

The strong golden thread of faith continued to weave through the drab tapestry. Its design of hope again spoke in Job 23:10.

"But He knows the way I take;
When He has tried me, I shall come forth as gold."

There are times when the depressed person can do nothing other than cling to God, when he cannot see any other hope or purpose in life. After major surgery a few years ago, I went through an excruciatingly painful depression. Pushing myself rather than resting, I was constantly exhausted. I hit the bottom emotionally. God seemed far away and I just couldn't reach Him. A friend gave me a mental picture to hang unto until the crisis had subsided.

Sometimes it is so foggy in the harbor of the San Francisco Bay that you cannot see the ships. You know they are there, you hear the fog horns. In order to see them you must wait until the fog lifts and the sun shines again.

So it is sometimes with God. I knew He was there because of the truth in His Word. I just had to wait for depression's fog to lift before I could see Him again.

Fourth, he remembered former days. In chapter 29, it is interesting to note what could have been a positive step for Job in his attempts to climb out of the doldrums. He remembered former days of God's blessing and nearness.

Oh that I were as in months gone by,
As in the days when God watched over me;
When His lamp shone over my head,
And by His light I walked through darkness;
As I was in the prime of my days,
When the friendship of God was over my tent;
When the Almighty was yet with me,
And my children were around me (Job 29:2–5).

The depressed person automatically remembers all the negative. He mulls over every problem in minute detail until even the tiniest difficulty grows into a mountain of impossibility and hopelessness. If he can begin to think of God's past goodness and care, he forces a faint glimmer of light to crack the seemingly impenetrable wall of despondency.

David gave us a good example.

O my God, my soul is in despair within me;
Therefore I remember Thee from the land of
the Jordan,
And the peaks of Hermon, from Mount Mizar
(Ps. 42:6).

David remembered victories and it helped him
climb out of the abyss of despair to hope in God.

Job began well, remembering God's former
goodness, but his clouded mind switched chan-
nels from God's glory to thinking about self.

When I went out to the gate of the city,
When I took my seat in the square;
The young men saw me and hid themselves,
And the old men arose and stood.
The princes stopped talking,
And put their hands on their mouths;
The voice of nobles was hushed,
And their tongue stuck to their palate.
For when the ear heard, it called me blessed;
And when the eye saw, it gave witness of me
(Job 29:7–11).

He continued, "I was an honest judge. I
helped those who were ready to perish. I caused
the widows' hearts to sing for joy." His goal was
to die quietly in his home after living a good,
long life. Three times he mentions God's name

in this chapter, but refers to "I" twenty times and "me" or "my" thirty-one times.

Job's mood rode high in chapter 29, remembering his former days with pride. But unlike David, he remembered his own greatness rather than God's, and such a foundation crumbled piteously in the face of Job's present grief.

His honor was replaced with ribald mockery, his esteem with spitting in his face, his protection with terror. He summed it all up with one last woeful lament against God.

And now my soul is poured out within me;
Days of affliction have seized me.
At night it pierces my bones within me,
And my gnawing pains take no rest.
By a great force my garment is distorted;
It binds me about as the collar of my coat.
He has cast me into the mire,
And I have become like dust and ashes.
I cry out to Thee for help,
but Thou dost not answer me (Job 30:16–20).

Lest we judge Job too severely, let us remember that he was not a man of stone, but of living flesh, crushed in the serpent's vice-grip.

God's Treatment

Job made one last attempt to prove his innocence in chapter 31. He proudly declared his innocence from lust, lying, coveting, unfair treatment of others, selfishness, greed, idolatry, desire for revenge, stealing, injustice, hiding his sins, murder. Job didn't understand the deceitfulness of his own heart.

The heart is more deceitful than all else
And is desperately sick;
Who can understand it? (Jer. 17:9).

He didn't realize that, even though he had not actively indulged in these things, he was capable of them all. Therefore, his adamant protestations of innocence revealed the sin of self-righteousness in Job, a serious sin with which God would deal. Perhaps one of God's purposes in turning Job over to Satan was to purify him.

I find it interesting that God did not mention Job's depression at all, nor did His spokesman, Elihu. This brings me to the conclusion that *Depression as an emotion is a symptom, not a cause.* We live in a day when psychology, psychiatry, religion, and drugs are all geared to make one "feel" better. But we need to deal with the root problem as God does. To confess depression as sin and attempt to break the habit applies only a Bandaid to the wound of hurting emotions. One needs to clean out the wound, suture the tissue back into place, and keep it clean while it heals.

I like what Hannah Whitehall Smith says in

the classic, *The Christian's Secret of a Happy Life.*
"The will is like a wise mother in a nursery; the
feelings are like a set of clamoring, crying children."[2]

God's concern and Satan's desire is to control
the mind and change the will. Human effort
cannot restore wounded or negative emotions.
Only God is able to accomplish that, operating
through a renewed mind and a responsive will.

With these thoughts in mind, let us examine
God's treatment. First, He listened until Job had
thoroughly expressed all the frustrations,
doubts, and accusations that boiled under his
self-righteous facade. Second, at the right time
God sent His forerunner, Elihu, to speak in His
behalf. Third, He captivated the attention of
Job's mind; and, last, He presented a true picture of His power contrasted with Job's weakness.

God listened to Job and allowed him time to
express himself with all the confusion of his
mixed-up emotions. Both the positive and negative spewed forth at random, from self-defense
to self-pity, to self-righteousness, to rejection of
God's dealings, to crying out to God as his deliverer. With free expression, the root cause eventually rose to the surface and could be dealt with
objectively.

A depressed person needs a listening ear, one

who will allow the flow of words to continue until the real issues eventually surface. They then can be dealt with appropriately. This takes time and patience for a family member, a friend, pastor, or counselor. Too often advice is given before the cause is clear, thus prolonging the symptoms and imbedding the cause a little deeper into its self-protective shell.

My husband has learned, by living with me, to be a tender and helpful listener. He has listened and listened as I have poured out my feelings of depression with all my subjective reactions and frustrations. When each torrent subsided to a trickle he offered objective, helpful insight leading me to finding answers in God's Word.

I no longer have to battle everything inside, keeping it there with the force of a bottle cork. Freely telling how it feels clears away the rubble so I can see reality and truth from God's perspective.

God sent a forerunner. A young man, Elihu, stood respectfully by, waiting for his chance to speak. Anger burned within him against Job who justified himself before God, and against the three older men who condemned Job though they had no answers.

Elihu made several important observations, revealing Job's true problem. First, he showed that Job had lack of the knowledge of God. Because God is sovereign, Job had no right to argue with Him (c. 34). God owes no man an explanation for His actions (32:13). Secondly, He is never wicked or unjust as Job had declared, because of His character as God (34:12). Third, Job had been wrong in assuming that God lacked concern for sin (34:7–9). Furthermore, he was arrogant, rebellious, and proud.

True, Job gave verbal assent to his involvement with human sin, but in a non-specific way (Job 7:21; 13:26). Confession involves specific naming of the sin and turning from it. Job had begged God to show him his sin so he could confess it. Elihu did just that.

Elihu pointed out some excellent advice for Job and for any suffering person.

Beware lest wrath entice you to scoffing.
Be careful, do not turn to evil;
For you have preferred this to affliction (Job 36:18, 21).

Job had scoffed against God and spoken evil of Him, resulting in deeper depression.

Elihu closed his challenge to Job with a beautiful glance of God's power portrayed in the elements, yet also His mercy available to needy man.

The Almighty—we cannot find Him;
He is exalted in power;
And He will not do violence to justice and
abundant righteousness (Job 37:23).

If Job could see God as God, omnipotent yet
merciful, and focus his pain-ridden thoughts on
the only source of help, his depression would
assuage. Herein, Elihu began the task of turning
Job's attention to the true character of God and
began the revelation which God Himself continued. His words evidently penetrated the
proud, self-righteous shell of Job, because he
had nothing to say in response, no self-defense
or retaliation.

God captivated the attention of Job's mind. As
Job sat in mute contemplation of Elihu's magnificent oratory in defense of God's character, a
little breeze blew dust in circles at his feet.
Higher and wider the circle blew until Job stared
in astonishment as the resonant voice of God
spoke from the whirlwind.

Who is this that darkens counsel
By words without knowledge?
Now gird up your loins like a man,
And I will ask you, and you instruct Me! (Job
38:2,3).

God captivated the attention of Job's mind, thus beginning the final phase of treatment.

God challenged Job to fight, probably an imagery from the ancient sport of belt-wrestling which was used as an ordeal in court also. One of the aims of belt-wrestling was to strip the opponent of his belt. It might take several falls to signify defeat.

God, the Creator, challenged His creature, the critic, to a test of wisdom. In doing so, Job gained new understanding of God's power, wisdom, strength, and sovereignty. Job's thoughts shifted from his own poverty and pain to a God in whom his faith could rest.

God revealed Himself basically in two ways: first in creation and nature and then in rule over wildlife.

Where were you when I laid the foundation of the earth!
Tell Me, if you have understanding.
Or who enclosed the sea with doors,
When bursting forth, it went out from the womb:
When I made a cloud its garment,
And thick darkness its swaddling band.
And I placed boundaries on it,
And I set a bolt and doors,
And I said, 'Thus far you shall come, but no farther;

And here shall your proud waves stop'? (Job
38:4, 8–11).
Where is the way that the light is divided,
Or the east wind scattered on the earth?
Who has cleft a channel for the flood,
Or a way for the thunderbolt;
To bring rain on a land without people,
On a desert without a man in it,
To satisfy the waste and desolate land,
And to make the seeds of grass to sprout? (Job
38:24–27).
Who sent out the wild donkey free?
And who loosed the bonds of the swift donkey,
To whom I gave the wilderness for a home,
And the salt land for his dwelling place? (Job
39:5, 6).
Is it by your understanding that the hawk soars,
Stretching his wings toward the south?
Is it at your command that the eagle mounts up,
And makes his nest on high? (Job 39:26, 27).

The first round of wrestling ended, God asked
Job if he was ready to admit defeat and yield to
Him (Job 40:2).

Job's submissive response indicated the beginning of his trek on the road to repentance.

Behold, I am insignificant; what can I reply to
Thee?
I lay my hand on my mouth (Job 40:4).

He was humbled by the manifestation of God's sovereignty, not a theological debate.

God presented a true picture of His power and of Job's weakness. A second time God spoke from the whirlwind, calling Job to another round of wrestling. This time He proved Job's incapability to judge the situation correctly because of his lack of ability to judge the wicked or to conquer animals created by God.

Will you really annul My judgment?
Will you condemn Me that you may be justified?
Or do you have an arm like God,
And can you thunder with a voice like His?
Adorn yourself with eminence and dignity;
And clothe yourself with honor and majesty.
Pour out the overflowings of your anger;
And look on everyone who is proud, and make him low.
Look on everyone who is proud, and humble him;
And tread down the wicked where they stand.
Hide them in the dust together;
Bind them in the hidden place.
Then I will also confess to you
That your own right hand can save you (Job 40:8–14).

If Job were not strong enough to battle victoriously over mere wicked men, surely he couldn't engage in combat with Satan, the real foe in this duel, and save himself. God graphically pointed out Job's weakness and need for the strength found only in Him. In his depression, Job had deprived himself of this source of strength because of his accusations against God and improper concept of himself.

"If you can't judge the wicked men, try wild animals," God went on to say. He chose two fierce examples commonly identified as the hippopotamus and the crocodile.

Behold now, Behemoth, which I made as well as you. . . .
Can anyone capture him when he is on watch,
With barbs can anyone pierce his nose? (Job 40:15, 24).
Can you draw out Leviathan with a fishhook? . . .
Lay your hand on him;
Remember the battle; you will not do it again! . . .
No one is so fierce that he dares to arouse him;
Who then is he that can stand before me? (Job 41:1, 8, 10).

God needed to speak no further. He had presented himself as creator, ruler, and sustainer of the universe, the earth, man, animals, and all of life. He claimed to be the only capable judge of wicked men, showing His justice, might, power, and sovereignty. He is God, and as God needs not to defend His actions or to be judged or criticized by man whom He created.

God's treatment for Job in his depressed, deplorable state concluded with a majestic and powerful display of His wisdom and strength. He had captivated Job's mind, turning his thoughts to Himself, and away from his suffering and debating his righteousness. Yet, He surely showed himself to be a caring God, concerned with the suffering of His child, by the fact that He condescended to personally communicate with Job out of the whirlwind. This fact melted Job's proud, defensive heart.

RESULTS OF THE TREATMENT

God's treatment for Job resulted in phenomenal happenings. Following Job's confession, God vindicated His name. Job found his deep heart-longing satisfied, and his character has been preserved through the centuries. Finally, Job experienced great reward for himself and his family.

Confession of Job's Mouth

The most important result is found in Job 42:5, 6.

I have heard of Thee by the hearing of the ear;
But now my eye sees Thee;
Therefore I retract,
And I repent in dust and ashes (Job 42:5, 6).

In seeing God as He is, Job saw himself in his loathsome sinfulness, bringing confession and repentance. By his surrender, he struck the death blow to Satan's accusation that he served God for his own advantages. At this point he was still in his near-death state and didn't understand that he was the victim of a confrontation between God and Satan, nor could he glimpse future blessing.

Notice that his confession was not for sin prior to his suffering. This would support the three friends' accusations. Nor did he confess his depression, but rather the foolish rebellion registered against God because of his suffering.

I know that Thou canst do all things,
And that no purpose of Thine can be thwarted.
'Who is this that hides counsel without knowledge?'
Therefore I have declared that which I did not understand,
Things too wonderful for me, which I did not know (Job 42:2, 3).

Job finally understood his proud, depraved nature, yet rejoiced in a fresh glimpse of God in His greatness and mercy. He received forgiveness and restoration of fellowship with God. Indeed, he realized a deeper intimacy with God, leading him to greater spiritual maturity.

Vindication of Job's Name

The second result was that God vindicated Job's name before his friends.

> And it came about after the Lord had spoken these words to Job, then the Lord said to Eliphaz the Temanite, "My wrath is kindled against you and against your two friends, because you have not spoken of Me what is right as My servant Job has (Job 42:7).

Because they did not confess their pride and cruel judgment of Job, God required them to offer sacrifices for their sin. God not only spoke words of commendation for Job, but gave him the mediator position of praying for his tormentors as they brought their animals for sacrifice. This added another positive result to Job's life, that of forgiving those who spoke so vehemently against him. Surely as Job prayed for them he experienced the freedom of forgiveness in his own soul.

Satisfaction of Job's Heart

Four times God referred to Job as "my servant." The deep heart-longing of Job for a personal relationship with the Almighty was satisfied. Job had the privilege of speaking to God face to face as he had cried out for.

Oh that I knew where I might find Him,
That I might come to His seat! (Job 23:3).

In confession, cleansing, and restored fellowship with God, the heart is satisfied. In God, not in anti-depressants or psychotherapy, is lasting healing for depression.

Preservation of Job's Character

Job's name has been preserved for all generations as the prime example of patience. "Behold, we count those blessed who endured. You have heard of the endurance of Job and have seen the outcome of the Lord's dealings, that the Lord is full of compassion and is merciful" (James 5:11).

How encouraging it is to think of this verse when we compare Job's struggles, confusion, questioning, and depression with our own!

Reward of Job's Family

The result of God's treatment of Job is found in 42:19. "And the Lord restored the fortunes of Job when he prayed for his friends, and the Lord increased all that Job had twofold" (Job 42:10). At this point Satan slunk away in sorry defeat, his battle for Job forever lost. Not only was Job's relationship with God established with greater knowledge and meaning, but God poured out physical blessings as well for His trusted "servant."

The concluding verses of this fascinating story read like a fairy-tale ending. "And he had seven sons and three daughters. And after this Job lived 140 years, and saw his sons, and his grandsons, four generations. And Job died, an old man and full of days" (Job 42:13, 16, 17).

As far as we know, God didn't explain to Job the real cause of his suffering. Having been lifted out of the quagmire of his depression by a magnificent revelation of the awesomeness of God, Job no longer cried out for understanding. He saw God for who He was, and saw himself in the reality of his sin, and the depression evaporated like the dew in the warmth of morning sun.

Is there victory today for depression caused from Satan and his enemy hosts? Sometimes he sneaks around and envelops a tired individual with crushing oppression, leaving that one feeling hopeless and depressed. James says, "Submit therefore to God. Resist the devil and he will flee from you" (James 4:7).

I remember teaching a particularly thrilling lesson to my ladies' Bible study. After the lesson a class member shared a problem with me. I was very objective about it all until I got home. Tired, and in a let-down mood, thoughts flashed across my mind in rapid succession.

"You're wasting your time teaching those ladies."

"They'll show interest for a while and then they won't bother to study any more."

"It's all Mickey-Mouse anyway."

I listened and became depressed. Then, I recognized the source of the oft-repeated cycle in my life. Satan can control my mind to think negatively; my emotions become depressed, and then it is easy for my will to fall and I act in negative ways.

Paul said: "For though we walk in the flesh, we do not war according to the flesh, for the weapons of our warfare are not of the flesh, but divinely powerful for the destruction of fortresses. We are destroying speculations and every lofty thing raised up against the knowledge of God, and we are taking every thought captive to the obedience of Christ" (II Cor. 10:3–5).

I chose to bring my thoughts captive to the obedience of Christ and busied myself by working on this manuscript. Satan's efforts were squelched—that time!

Sometimes oppression is felt like a heavy, nameless cloud, smothering out the very air we breathe. Sometimes it is through inordinate tension, the feeling of a volcano inside about to erupt. When my husband was a pastor, Saturdays were important days at our home. It was prime time for the enemy to move in causing indefinable chaos and strain for our family. The conclusion of such a day would find me in the stronghold of depression. We need to be alert, recognizing that the victory is ours through the finished work of Jesus Christ on the cross.

"Since then the children share in flesh and blood, He Himself likewise also partook of the same, that through death He might render powerless him who had the power of death, that is, the devil; and might deliver those who through fear of death were subject to slavery all their lives" (Heb. 2:14, 15).

There is freedom in Jesus Christ!

---

1. Leonard Cammer, *Up From Depression* (New York: Simon and Schuster, 1969), pp. 52, 53.
2. Hannah Whitehall Smith, *The Christian's Secret of a Happy Life* (Westwood, NJ: Fleming H. Revell, 1968), p. 85.

5

FRUSTRATED GOALS
Rx: Hannah

More than anything else, Hannah longed for a child. To a Hebrew woman, barrenness was synonymous with God's judgment or displeasure. And the faint hope of becoming the mother of the promised Messiah burned in the heart of every Israelite woman. Hannah was reminded continuously of her empty body as she watched Peninnah, Elkanah's second wife, mother her sons and daughters.

Daily Peninnah scorned, mocked, and derided Hannah because she had no children. Because Elkanah loved Hannah the most, Peninnah's resentment flourished. Her stinging remarks and constant tormenting provoked Hannah bitterly.

Year after year Hannah endured affliction from hostile, sarcastic Peninnah. She languished under the pain of her own infertility and merciless attacks of her tormentor, until "she wept and would not eat (I Sam. 1:7). Hannah was depressed.

STATEMENT OF DEPRESSION

Elkanah, Hannah's devoted husband, uttered the statement of her depression. "Hannah, why do you weep and why do you not eat and why is your heart sad? Am I not better to you than ten sons?" (I Sam. 1:8).

Elkanah's love and tenderness did not alleviate Hannah's oppressed spirit and burden of heart.

CAUSES OF DEPRESSION

The cause of Hannah's depression may be stated as "frustrated goals." Lack of fulfillment, shattered hopes, or broken dreams developed in a person's mind, can cause a reactive depression as real as in the case of grief or displacement. This was the reason Hannah was sad and would not eat. Her depressive state had progressed over a period of years to the point where she lost interest in her surroundings and found life joyless and painful. Even a loving, considerate husband could not ease her suffering. "And it hap-

pened year after year, as often as she went up to
the house of the Lord, she would provoke her,
so she wept and would not eat" (I Sam. 1:7).
Unbearable taunting from jealous Peninnah
heightened Hannah's unhappiness.

TREATMENT OF DEPRESSION

Hannah initiated treatment for herself by ven-
tilating her feelings to God in prayer. God completed the process of healing for Hannah with a
promise.

Hannah's Prayer

"And she, greatly distressed, prayed to the
Lord and wept bitterly" (I Sam. 1:10).

Why is it difficult for distressed individuals to
be honest before God? Why do I often bury my
real need under a covering of pretty phrases?
Too often we pray pious words and spiritual
sounding platitudes, while God desires aban-
donment of our souls and transparency of our
need. Only then can He intervene to meet that
need in His own way. The Pharisee's self-
righteous prayer bounced off the ceiling of the
temple, while the candid, broken publican's
prayer was heard and answered (Luke 18:10–
13).

It is important also to note that Hannah went directly to God, the only One who can ultimately satisfy the troubled heart. In seeking to help a depressed friend or family member, a listening ear benefits greatly. However, the eventual goal should be to turn the attention of the sufferer toward objective truth found in God and His Word.

To listen with a sympathetic ear for hours, days, and weeks to reiterated woes, without offering a solid foundation where the wavering feet of a depressed wanderer can come to rest, is to offer no help at all. Aimless listening allows the grooves in his sorrowful record to be cut deeper.

God's Promise

Associated with Hannah's prayer was a vow. In essence she prayed, "Oh Lord, if you will indeed notice my affliction and hear me, and give me a son, then I will give him back to you. He shall be a Nazarite set apart to serve you as long as he lives."

Her vow revealed the sincerity of her heart and deep commitment to God. And God heard her prayer.

As Eli, the priest, saw her lips moving but making no sound, he roughly accused her of drunkenness.

"But Hannah answered and said, "No, my Lord, I am a woman oppressed in spirit; I have drunk neither wine nor strong drink, but I have poured out my soul before the Lord. Do not consider your maidservant as a worthless woman; for I have spoken until now out of my great concern and provocation" (I Sam. 1:15, 16).

Eli then encouraged her. "Go in peace; and may the God of Israel grant your petition that you have asked of Him" (I Sam. 1:17).

God sent hope for Hannah through His servant Eli.

RESULTS OF HANNAH'S DEPRESSION

Hannah's depression due to frustrated goals, drove her to God in unbridled dependence. There were three results from this encounter. First, Hannah matured spiritually. Second, God's plan for a new priestly family was realized. Third, Hannah was blessed with an unexpected family.

Spiritual Growth for Hannah

Hannah accepted Eli's words as a promise from God. She went her way and ate her dinner with a happy face. Her faith in God's promise to give her the desire of her heart, a son, dispelled the cloud of depression. Now Peninnah's stabbing words would no longer penetrate her wounded spirit. God's promise was her shield.

As with Hannah, times of depression have caused some of my greatest spiritual growth.

"I do not know all the joys and trials waiting future days ... but I know that God has a purpose for me to fill." My words were spoken confidently to the captive audience of our new congregation. Illness was the furthest thought from my mind.

Every ounce of physical strength began to drain from my body until eventually I collapsed on the sofa. And the boring days dragged on. My accomplishments consisted of preparing easy meals and somehow getting the laundry done, one dreary load at a time.

"God," I cried. "Why have you done this to me? I have a book to write, a house to decorate, a trip to take. Don't you care at all?" Cycles of struggling trust, frantic rebellion, loneliness, and depression faded into a drab kaleidoscope of gray and hopeless days. Months later I discovered a faint glimmer of light. God had been trying to teach me an important truth, but I was a slow learner.

I came to see how easy it is for my interests and activities to take priority over my relationship with God. He is my delight, the source of my fulfillment and my joy. In order to allow this intellectual knowledge to filter down to my practice, He removed all the competition for an extended time.

He gave me a new understanding of His person. He is good. That is His character and He can operate in no other way. He was good to me when He removed the frills and trappings of an active life; the social gatherings, the entertaining, writing a book, sewing a new dress, decorating our home. Gently and persistently He brought me to a place of submission to Him in a new way, to glorify Him in physical weakness.

"Lord, if you want me to spend the rest of my life with just this amount of strength, I am willing. Give me wisdom to reorganize my lifestyle and glorify you in it."

My frustrated goals resulted in depression. But it no longer plagued my still weary body when I saw the truth of His person and submitted to Him afresh.

God does not always answer our prayer in the way we ask. But He does promise to give us the desires of our hearts. "Delight yourself in the Lord; and He will give you the desires of your heart" (Ps. 37:4). And if we are delighting in Him, He will either grant our petitions or change our desires. Either way, we'll know contentment.

God's Plan Realized in a Son

It is beautiful to see how God, in response to a broken woman's plea, accomplished His purpose far beyond what Hannah would have imagined.

"Now the sons of Eli were worthless men; they did not know the Lord" (I Sam. 2:12). Immoral and cruel, they abused the sacrificial system for their own selfish gain. Eli had failed to discipline them.

One day God sent a prophet to Eli with a message. "God says to you, I chose your father's house to be my priests forever. But you have despised my sacrifices and offerings, honoring your sons before me. Therefore you have lost your priestly privileges and as a sign your wicked sons Hophni and Phinehas shall both die on the same day. But I will raise up an obedient, faithful priest instead." (I Sam. 2:30–35, my paraphrase.)

God prepared Samuel to be that faithful priest. "Thus Samuel grew and the Lord was with him and let none of his words fail. And all Israel from Dan even to Beersheba knew that Samuel was confirmed as a prophet of the Lord" (I Sam. 3:19, 20).

Hannah's faith in God was confirmed. Her mother's heart rejoiced daily that God had a place of high honor chosen for her son—the result of a depressed woman's prayer.

Reward of Unexpected Family

Little Samuel played around Hannah's feet as she joyfully completed the day's tasks. As she watched him grow, she taught him of God's love and His Word. Her heart was content.

The day of fulfilling her vow drew near when she would leave her only son at the temple. She prepared him well, and stilled any anxiety and prelude to loneliness by reminding herself of the faithfulness of God. He was her exultation. He would fill the empty house with His presence and her heart would never be empty again.

Hannah had learned to delight in God. Keeping her vow, she took Samuel to the temple, still a very young boy, and presented him to Eli along with a bull for sacrifice.

"Sir, remember me? I am the woman who came to pray. I prayed for a son and the Lord gave me my request. Here he is, dedicated to the Lord as long as he lives." What faith Hannah exhibited! She left her child at the temple, visiting him only once a year.

Year by year, Hannah returned with her husband to worship God with the yearly sacrifice and to bring Samuel a new coat. I wonder, as she

kissed him goodbye each year, if she ever regret-
ted making her vow. The Lord kept Hannah
from regrets or undue loneliness by giving her
three more sons and two daughters. Hannah's
life was complete and her heart was full.

Depression due to frustrated goals must be
treated by bringing those goals into line with
God's plan for our lives. We need to communicate freely with Him the desires of our heart.
How delicate is the thread dividing our hanging
on to our own wills and giving in to His. Only
He knows when the work of submission at each
particular encounter is complete. Freedom from
depression is the result of leaving the choice to
Him.

6

UNCONFESSED SIN

R X: Jonah

"Jonah, go to Nineveh with my message of judgment. The wickedness rises repulsively before me."

Jonah, hearing God's command, packed his bags and hurried to the seaport of Joppa. He joined bustling sailors and jostling passengers, paid his fare, and climbed aboard a ship headed for Tarshish, directly opposite the direction of Nineveh. With a false sense of peace he fell asleep in the hold, glad to be away from God's presence and His command.

Soon the gentle wind blew angry blasts. She buffeted the struggling sails and whipped the waves into a frenzy as they lashed against the laden ship. Harried, frightened sailors prayed to their gods, bailed out the sea water and threw the cargo overboard. Nothing helped and Jonah slept on.

Finally the captain discovered him. "How can

you sleep at a time like this? Call out to your God for deliverance."

But Jonah wasn't in a praying mood.

"Let's draw straws," the sailors decided, "to see who is to blame for this catastrophe."

Jonah drew the shortest straw and was forced to confess his disobedience to God. "Just throw me overboard and the sea will be calm."

Unable to row against the tempestuous waves, they had no recourse but to follow Jonah's advice. Into the dark waters he plunged, bringing instant calm to the troubled sea.

"And the Lord appointed a great fish to swallow Jonah, and Jonah was in the stomach of the fish three days and three nights" (Jonah 1:17).

Surrounded by slimy walls, with no way of escape, Jonah cried out to God for deliverance, confessing his disobedience. "While I was fainting away, I remembered the Lord; And my prayer came to Thee, into Thy holy temple. Those who regard vain idols forsake their faithfulness. But I will sacrifice to Thee with the voice of thanksgiving. That which I have vowed I will pay. Salvation is from the Lord" (Jonah 2:7–9).

What a relief Jonah must have felt as he was ejected rather unceremoniously onto the beach! Keeping his promise, he traveled immediately to Nineveh with new power and determination.

"God will overthrow your city in forty days."

Jonah preached up and down the streets of this great city in Assyria.

His preaching produced phenomenal response. From the king down to the lowliest servant, each man, woman, and beast covered themselves in sackcloth and sat among the ashes in repentance. They tasted no food and drank no water as all cried out to the God of Israel for mercy.

"When God saw their deeds, that they turned from their wicked way, then God relented concerning the calamity which He had declared He would bring upon them. And He did not do it" (Jonah 3:10).

STATEMENT OF DEPRESSION

Jonah was not prepared for such overwhelming response to his sermon of imminent judgment. "Therefore now, O Lord, please take my life from me, for death is better to me than life" (Jonah 4:3).

Jonah plunged headlong into depression's doleful pit.

CAUSES OF JONAH'S DEPRESSION

There is only one cause for Jonah's depression found in a study of the book bearing his name, and that is sin. First, he indulged the sin of his prejudice and lack of love toward a race different from his own. Then, he lashed out in anger against God. Pride and selfishness are also noticed. The result was depression and longing to die. The guilt of unconfessed sin resulted in depression.

Prejudice and Hatred

Being a staunch Israelite, Jonah hated the heathen around him. Nineveh, a city in Assyria, was especially hated because of the threat of attack from that country. The fear was not unfounded because Assyria, in fact, did arise as a cruel enemy which overthrew and destroyed Israel (II Kings 17:7, 18).

Nevertheless, God had commanded Israel to be a light to the Gentiles, to cause them to know the true God, and to turn from idolatry. In disobedience and religious pride, Israel kept their knowledge of God to themselves, not caring about the lost and dying nations around them.

"And he prayed to the Lord and said, "Please Lord, was not this what I said while I was still in my own country? Therefore, in order to forestall this I fled to Tarshish, for I knew that Thou art a gracious and compassionate God, slow to anger and abundant in lovingkindness, and one who relents concerning calamity" (Jonah 4:2).

The true reason Jonah fled was his unconcern and lack of love for a nation. He knew God's promise of judgment often carried with it a conditional clause. Punishment would be restrained if there were repentance. Jonah's hatred burned with vengeance. He actually would have enjoyed watching Nineveh endure God's wrath.

Pride and Anger

Because events did not transpire as he had wished, Jonah became angry with God. "But it greatly displeased Jonah, and he became angry" (Jonah 4:1).

Jonah looked at theological truth, the forgiving and gracious character of God. Instead of rejoicing in the truth and drawing closer to God, Jonah reacted sinfully, causing a gap in his relationship with God.

Perhaps Jonah's pride also made him angry. After all, he had vociferously proclaimed doom in forty days. Now that God had changed His mind, who would believe his prophecies ever again? In sulking petulance Jonah stalked to the east of Nineveh, built himself a booth and sat down to watch. Maybe God would yet destroy the city.

TREATMENT OF JONAH'S DEPRESSION

In treating Jonah's problem, God did two things: He directly confronted the cause of the depression, and He provided an object lesson to teach Jonah.

Cause Confronted

In this particular case, God offered no sympathetic understanding, no time to talk things over, or to meet his needs. He rather bluntly approached Jonah with the basic issue.

And the Lord said, "Do you have good reason to be angry?" (Jonah 4:4).

It is significant that God was specific in naming the sin. Jonah's guilt was real and the only cure was repentance. True repentance involves confession, agreeing with God that it is sin, and turning from that sin.

Depression can also result from false guilt. This is guilt that arises from a feeling of having committed some sin, but we're not sure what. It could be a result of satanic oppression. The enemy of our souls loves to heap accusations upon us, involving many vague wrongs. He beats us down with feelings of guilt, making us ineffective for God.

False guilt also arises from violating standards or expectations of parents, peers, or of our own, which are not God's standards. Some of us develop hyperactive consciences because of legalistic backgrounds or strict rules and regulations that go beyond God's requirements.

Victory over satanically induced false guilt is found in Jesus Christ. God deals specifically, usually with one sin at a time. He is interested in conviction and bringing to repentance, not in causing depression and despair. Recognizing the source, submitting ourselves to God, and resisting Satan's attack through Jesus Christ, causes Him to flee (James 4:7; Heb. 2:14, 15).

False guilt caused by unrealistic expectations that are not from God, needs to be recognized as such and rejected. This is accomplished as we get to know God's Word, His standards for holiness, and the freedom that is ours in Jesus Christ (Gal. 5:1).

In the case of definite sin, we must be bold enough to call sin, sin. There is no cure in hiding the root cause and looking for easement from depression by blaming our temperament, background, or environment. Use of anti-depressants, counseling, and psychoanalysis at times brings temporary relief, but until the question of sin is uncovered and confessed, relief is merely an elusive dream.

Cause Demonstrated

God followed Jonah to his booth east of Nineveh, saw him sitting and sulking, and began to teach him a much needed lesson. Miraculously, a plant with broad and shiny leaves sprouted up. It spread welcome shade over Jonah as he sweltered in the sun. All day Jonah rejoiced in the beautiful shade of the plant.

The next morning a squiggly worm attacked the plant, causing it to wither and die. As the morning sun rose high, God sent a scorching east wind and together they buffeted poor Jonah until he became faint and cried out for relief in death.

Now God reiterated His question. "Do you have good reason to be angry about the plant?" Jonah was still angry. "I have good reason to be angry, even to death" (Jonah 4:9). He was angry because of the physical discomfort he endured.

Again the Lord spoke to Jonah. "You feel sorry for the plant. You neither planted it nor caused it to grow. It came up in one night and was gone the next. Shouldn't I have mercy on this great city, Nineveh, where more than 120,000 children live, besides the adults and living animals?"

It was as if God said, "How can you be more

concerned for a plant and your own comfort, than for living, lost people who need to know me?"

God was finished, leaving Jonah to face his sinful attitude.

RESULTS OF JONAH'S DEPRESSION

There are two results noted. First, there is the assumed repentance of Jonah; and second, we have an illustration for today of the role of sin in causing depression.

Opportunity to Repent

The dramatic story of Jonah ends abruptly, making you want to turn the page to find out what happened next. How did Jonah respond? We are not told. But if one believes that Jonah is the author of the book, as is the view held by conservative scholars, we may assume that Jonah repented of his sins of anger and prejudice, selfishness and pride. He was thus delivered from his wish to die and his depression. Otherwise he would not have been willing to expose his weakness in writing this story.

Illustration for Today

Any underlying, continued unconfessed sin can cause depression. Modern society, even Christians, run to psychiatrists, counselors, and sympathetic friends to find alleviation for their depression.

"I wish a semi-truck would crash into me as I drive home and kill me."

A young friend squeezed these words from her tormented mind. She was depressed. Uncovering the cause exposed the ugliness of sin. She had been engaging in the sin of lying. The first time her conscience pricked her, she ignored it. The habit became easier and fellowship with God was broken. Later she cried out to Him in a time of need and He did not hear. "If I regard wickedness in my heart, the Lord will not hear" (Ps. 66:18).

Adding feelings of rejection to her tortured soul, she fell into despondency. Sin dragged her downward to depression.

Sin may be resentment toward a family member, immorality plaguing from the past, or covetousness—that inordinate desire for possessions or people to which we have no right. Paul said that he had not known the sin of coveting unless the law had said, "You shall not covet" (Rom. 7:7). Then he realized coveting of every kind in his life.

The list is as endless and as personal as the sin that haunts each particular individual. I have known the deadening weight of depression resulting from sin I refused to admit. How it presses down the heart, distorts the thinking, and clouds each waking hour with gloom and sadness! Depression, resulting from sin affects the body as well as the mind.

When I kept silent about my sin, my body wasted away
Through my groaning all day long.
For day and night Thy hand was heavy upon me;
My vitality was drained away as with the fever-heat of summer (Ps. 32:3, 4).

Disconsolate sighs escape the mouths of disgruntled homemakers in check-out counters of grocery stores. Unhappy, expressionless eyes stare from somber faces of professional men and blue-collar workers alike. Woe-be-gone teenagers despair under merciless melancholy, and the suicide rate rises. In our sophisticated society which rejects the absolutes of God's Word and extolls sin of every description, depression soars to epidemic proportions.

David responded,

I acknowledged my sins to Thee,
And my iniquity I did not hide;
I said, "I will confess my transgressions to the
Lord";
and Thou didst forgive the guilt of my sin (Ps.
32:5).

And he found relief for the physical and emotional torment resulting from sin in his life.

7

JOB PRESSURE

Rx: Moses

Across arid wasteland ambled a solitary figure, his rough cloak tossed over his shoulder, shepherd staff in hand. Bleating, satisfied sheep followed along, nibbling a shrub here, a piece of parched grass there. Wandering through desolate places, the shepherd searched for a fresh waterhole.

Suddenly his eyes brightened, his step hurried. What strange thing transpired before his astonished eyes? A bush on fire, yet it wasn't consumed! He picked his way closer to investigate.

"Moses," spoke a voice from the fire.

"Here I am," he tremblingly replied.

"Take off your shoes, Moses. The ground you're standing on is holy."

Transfixed, Moses stooped to untie his sandals and stepped barefooted onto the hot sand.

"I am the God of your father, the God of

Abraham, the God of Isaac, and the God of Jacob" (Exod. 3:6).

Moses was afraid and buried his face in his cloak. The Lord continued speaking from the burning bush.

"I have heard the cries of my people suffering in Egypt and am come down to deliver them. I want to take them out to a land flowing with milk and honey. You will go to Pharoah to bring my people out of Egypt."

Moses, out of a deep sense of fear and insecurity, debated with God. After all, he had tried that once forty years ago and had failed miserably. Out in the wilderness, communing with stupid sheep, he had lost all the confidence of an Egyptian trained son, second in line to the Pharaoh. Eventually he conceded to obey, only after God promised to send his brother Aaron along as his spokesman.

This timid, cowering, servant of God threatened Pharaoh as the plagues fell in cataclysmic sequence on the wicked Egyptians (see Exod. 7–12). The ultimate disaster occurred as the Lord passed through Egypt, slaying the first-born son in every Egyptian family. Pharaoh and the people compelled the Israelites to leave before death devoured them all.

Hurriedly in the dark of night the people fled. Bleating sheep and bawling steers, sleepy children and anxious grandmothers hastened from their homes into the starlit desert and toward the Red Sea.

As morning dawned, Pharaoh shouted, "What have I done to let them go? Who will serve us now?"

Gathering together his army, he rushed out to overtake his slaves and drive them back. Horses and chariots, marching soldiers and cavalry men sped across the land, blasting clouds of dust into the air.

Camping by the sea, the people of Israel had stopped to rest after the long journey. Suddenly their peace jolted to panic as the dust clouds blew closer, and Pharaoh's army surged into view. They cried out to Moses in their fright.

"Is it because there were no graves in Egypt that you have taken us away to die in the wilderness? Why have you dealt with us in this way, bringing us out of Egypt? Is this not the word that we spoke to you in Egypt, saying, 'Leave us alone that we may serve the Egyptians'? For it would have been better for us to serve the Egyptians than to die in the wilderness" (Exod. 14:11, 12).

God miraculously parted the sea in response to Moses' outstretched rod, and the multitude crossed over on dry ground. Egyptians plunged in after them. Chariot wheels swerved and rebelled against their riders. Finally, the walls of water tumbled in upon them, destroying them all.

Moses, a shepherd of obedient, contented sheep found himself the leader of a rebellious, disobedient mob of Israelites, crossing the wilderness toward Canaan.

STATEMENT OF DEPRESSION

Grumbling, murmuring, and complaining characterized the children of Israel entrusted to Moses' care. Patiently Moses bore the brunt of their ungratefulness and sin until the pressure became unbearable and he became depressed.

"I alone am not able to carry all this people, because it is too burdensome for me. So if Thou art going to deal thus with me, please kill me at once, if I have found favor in Thy sight, and do not let me see my wretchedness" (Num. 11:14, 15).

CAUSES OF MOSES' DEPRESSION

The major cause of Moses' depression was stress—job pressure. He also experienced an emotional let-down after a high, he lost sight of God's power, and he forgot God's promises.

Job Pressure

Moses seems to be the type of personality that could take a great deal of pressure. He was patient, enduring, and not easily provoked. God said, "Now the man Moses was very meek, above all the men which were upon the face of the earth" (Num. 12:3).

He surely had one of the most difficult jobs ever assigned to one man, leading a vast multitude of men, women, children, and livestock across the desert from the Red Sea to the land of Canaan; a multitude of ungrateful, critical complainers (Exod. 12:37, 38).

At Marah, the people thirsted, but the water was bitter. "So the people grumbled at Moses, saying, "What shall we drink?" (Exod. 15:24).

Moses cried out to the Lord. God showed him a tree to toss into the water and it became sweet.

A few days later, their food supplies depleted, they grumbled against Moses again. "Would that we had died by the Lord's hand in the land of Egypt, when we sat by the pots of meat, when we ate bread to the full; for you have brought us out into this wilderness to kill this whole assembly with hunger" (Exod. 16:3).

And so they murmured, grumbled, and complained throughout the journey—across the wilderness of Sin, where God sent manna from heaven for food, through Rephidim, where

Moses struck the rock and sweet, sparkling water bubbled forth to satisfy their thirst. From morning to night he listened to their problems, giving counsel and direction from God.

Besides the daily burden of his griping followers, he also fought a battle with enemy Amalekites along the way.

At times the pressure mounted to unbearable heights. Aaron, his own brother and fellow-leader, made a golden calf to worship while Moses was with God receiving His law. Immorality and debauchery raged. Moses burned with anger at the idolatrous revelry, yet he interceded with God on their behalf (Exod. 32, 33).

Three days after they left Sinai, where Moses received the law and talked with God, the grumbling began again. "Who will give us meat to eat? We remember the fish which we used to eat free in Egypt, the cucumbers and the melons and the leeks and the onions and the garlic, but now our appetite is gone. There is nothing at all to look at except this manna" (Num. 11:4–6).

Moses had had it! Their greedy desire for meat and scorn for God's provision struck the final blow. He became angry with the people, and then depressed.

Every person has a built-in pressure barometer. Some, like Moses, can endure a great deal of stress before the valve explodes, causing depression or other emotional reactions. Others already operate at a high level of tension and need, by determination and planning, to keep the level down to prevent disorientation, anxiety or depression. Stress, prolonged and beyond an individual's capability, causes depression.

Emotional Let-down

Like Elijah, Moses gives us an example of a natural let-down feeling after an emotionally stimulating experience.

Moses had been on the mountain with God. Over a twelve-month period, he personally communed with God. "The Lord used to speak to Moses face to face, just as a man speaks to his friend" (Exod. 33:11a). So great was God's glory demonstrated through Moses, that his face shone, requiring him to wear a veil when speaking to the people (Exod. 34:29–35).

Basking in the memory of his personal encounter with the living God, Moses was not prepared for the shock of his return to the mundane. Only three days after leaving the mountain of God's holiness, the people complained again and Moses could no longer cope with them. In his time of emotional let-down, the seed of depression found fertile soil. It quickly sprouted and blossomed, choking out the fruit of right-eousness, which is joy.

Lost Sight of God's Power

Because Moses became angry, he lost sight of God's power. "Where am I to get meat to give to all this people? For they weep before me, saying, 'Give us meat that we may eat!'" (Num. 11:13).

Moses momentarily forgot that God had sent manna from the skies, bubbled water out of a rock, and sweetened the bitter stream with a fallen tree. He could have asked God as in times past and watched God provide. He was not thinking clearly and therefore assumed an impossible task for his own. The pressure caused him to be depressed. In the light of God's power, a provision of meat would have been easily accomplished. If only he had remembered!

God's Promises Forgotten

Just a few weeks before, God had promised Moses that He would go with him to lead the people into Canaan (Exod. 33:12–17). Moses forgot God's words and assumed the responsibility for himself. "I alone am not able to carry all this people, because it is too burdensome for me" (Num. 11:14).

The pressure was too great for Moses alone.

God had never intended Moses to carry out this tremendous task with his own abilities, but only in the strength and power of the Lord-God Himself. Moses had forgotten!

Pastors become depressed in their ministries because they forget God's promise, "Faithful is He who calls you, and He also will bring it to pass" (I Thess. 5:24). Harried wives become depressed as they assume multiple responsibilities of home and job, of community projects and church duties. Only a human dynamo could accomplish it all and the pressure causes depression. They forget that the promise of rest is theirs if they submit themselves to God's will for their lives, rather than submitting to unreasonable standards of a chaotic world.

"Come to Me, all who are weary and heavy laden, and I will give you rest. Take My yoke upon you, and learn from Me, for I am gentle and humble in heart; and you shall find rest for your souls. For my yoke is easy, and My load is light" (Matt. 11:28–30).

TREATMENT FOR MOSES

God's treatment for Moses in his depressed state is very encouraging. First of all, He understood the problem, and, second, He solved the problem. His solution involved two aspects. He met Moses' need, and He judged Israel, the source of the problem.

Problem Understood

God understood Moses' frustration, unhappiness, and complaint against Israel. God Himself reacted with anger and frustration on more than one occasion. Following their sin with the golden calf He threatened to leave them and send an angel instead. "And I will send an angel before you . . . to a land flowing with milk and honey; for I will not go up in your midst, because you are an obstinate people, lest I destroy you on the way" (Exod. 33:2, 3).

Later He threatened to destroy them and make a nation of Moses. His anger at their rebellion burned again when they refused to believe that He could take them into the Promised Land (Num. 14:27).

He subsequently destroyed the grumblers in the wilderness and allowed only their children to enter. Yes, God understood Moses' legitimate frustration and depression with this obnoxious, disobedient people.

God also understands when you and I are depressed. He cares about the hopelessness, the despair, the feelings of futility. Jesus Christ felt the devastating emotion of depression as He approached the Garden of Gethsemane, and the horrors of this final battle with all the powers of darkness. Mark tells us, "And He took with Him Peter and James and John, and began to be very distressed and troubled. And He said to them, My soul is deeply grieved to the point of death; remain here and keep watch" (Mark 14:33, 34).

Later as He hung on the cross, the agonizing cry exploded from His parched lips. "My God, My God, why hast Thou forsaken Me?" (Mark 15:34). He felt in the deepest sense the emotions experienced by the depressed, yet without sin.

"Therefore, He had to be made like His brethren in all things, that He might become a merciful and faithful high priest in things pertaining to God, to make propitiation for the sins of the people" (Heb. 2:17).

Jesus, the Son of Man, felt anger, loneliness, grief, and sadness. He understands when we feel depressed. It is not the emotion that is the problem, but how we react to the emotion. Do we allow it to control us, causing sin, or do we take the opportunity to develop a closer relationship with God? The writer to the Hebrews sums it up beautifully. "For we do not have a high priest who cannot sympathize with our weaknesses, but one who has been tempted in all things as we are, yet without sin" (Heb. 4:15).

Moses experienced the understanding of God in his time of depression.

Problem Solved

God didn't scold Moses for his depression, or belittle him for his incompetence. He just stepped in to solve the problem. First of all, He divided the responsibility among seventy elders of Israel, giving them the Holy Spirit also to accomplish the tremendous task of leading the army of Israelites. "Then I will come down and speak with you there, and I will take of the Spirit who is upon you, and will put Him upon them; and they shall bear the burden of the people with you, so that you shall not bear it all alone" (Num. 11:17).

God wants us to recognize His strength and ability to meet our needs. Sometimes the only way to be stripped of our own self-effort and confidence in the flesh, is to be brought up against a problem that is too big for us to handle. If, finding ourselves there, we, like Moses, cry out to God, He responds to meet that need.

David shows us over and over in the Psalms the sufficiency of God to deliver from stress.

In my distress I called upon the Lord,
And cried to my God for help;

He heard my voice out of His temple,
And my cry for help before Him came into His
ears.
He sent from on high, He took me;
He drew me out of many waters.
He delivered me from my strong enemy,
And from those who hated me, for they were
too mighty for me.
They confronted me in the day of my calamity,
But the Lord was my stay.
He brought me forth also into a broad place;
He rescued me, because He delighted in me (Ps.
18:6, 16–19).

The arrival at the state where we must say,
"Unless God moves in to work in this situation,
I am finished; it is hopeless," is a good place to
be. Because that is precisely when God is given
the green light to move ahead and work in our
behalf in miraculous ways. God never forces
Himself into our lives. He waits for us to recognize our helplessness and to rely on His re-
sourcefulness.

Second, God judged Israel, the source of
Moses' difficulty. They cried for meat, ungrateful for God's provision of manna.

On the wind of His breath, the Lord brought
quail in from the sea, so much that they covered
an area of two-days' journey, thirty-six inches

deep. The greedy Israelites gathered the quails, dressed them and spread them out to dry. Before the first bite had been chewed God's anger burned against His troublesome people and He struck them with a plague.

God's judgment on the people vindicated Moses. He had legitimate cause for his anger and frustration, therefore God had compassion on Moses. Because Israel's attitudes were sinful and totally unjustified, God punished them.

When stress of job, unreasonable people, trials, and calamities press in upon us, threatening to drive us to despair, we can remember Moses and be helped. We need to cry out to God, who loves to bring comfort and solve problems for His trusting children.

Give the problem and the people involved, up to God. He is the righteous judge. Paul reminds us of this. "Never take your own revenge, beloved, but leave room for the wrath of God, for it is written, Vengeance is Mine, I will repay, says the Lord" (Rom. 12:19).

RESULTS FOLLOWING TREATMENT

There are two results noted in Moses' life following his bout with depression. He continued in his leadership position effectively, and God recorded his outstanding epitaph.

Continued Leadership

Moses was faced with a choice. He could have allowed his depression to control him, leading him into self-pity and complete incompetency in his work. God would have been forced then to put him on the shelf and raise up another leader. In his choosing to cry out to God, he allowed God to work in his behalf. Help was sent, alleviating the inordinate job pressure, and also the state of depression.

Moses continued as the leader of this rebellious mob. He stood against the criticism of his family, the leaders of the congregation, and the multitudes. He interceded on their behalf in the face of God's anger for their refusal to enter the land. He led them patiently through forty years of wilderness wanderings. Even when Moses sinned in disobedience and anger, he patiently bore his punishment in not being able to enter the Promised Land. He showed concern for the people rather than his own loss.

"May the Lord, the God of the spirits of all flesh, appoint a man over the congregation, who will go out and come in before them, and who will lead them out and bring them in, that the congregation of the Lord may not be like sheep which have no shepherd" (Num. 27:16, 17).

Moses' prayer for his wayward sheep demonstrated his leadership ability and spiritual maturity.

Outstanding Epitaph

Moses had no ordinary funeral. One last trek into the mountain with God led him to Mount Nebo, to the top of Pisgah. He gazed down over Jericho and across the land of promise, flowing with milk and honey.

"Now you have seen it," said God. "But you may not enter." And there Moses died. It was as though his communion with God suddenly left his physical body and resumed from his spiritual body. We are told that God conducted the funeral and buried him in the land of Moab, but no one ever found the burial spot.

Moses' epitaph, written by God Himself, is not confined to a stone in a dreary graveyard, but is engraved in the living Word of God to be read by countless generations.

"Since then no prophet has risen in Israel like Moses, whom the Lord knew face to face, for all the signs and wonders which the Lord sent him to perform in the land of Egypt against Pharaoh, all his servants, and all his land, and for all the mighty power and for all the great terror which Moses performed in the sight of all Israel" (Deut. 34:10–12).

Recorded history bears out God's testimony of Moses. Throughout Scripture Moses is revered and honored by the prophets, the apostles, and the Savior Himself. He formed a picture of Christ in the Old Testament as deliverer. "And as Moses lifted up the serpent in the wilderness, even so must the Son of Man be lifted up" (John 3:14).

He was also given as an example of faith (Heb. 11:23–29). Moses was one of the greatest men who ever lived, even though he experienced depression. Meeting God in his need, the problem became a tool in drawing him closer to God in dependence and trust.

What shall I do then when pressures of life push me to the brink of depression? It is helpful for me to remember that there are God-sized problems, husband-sized problems, and wife-sized problems. When I assume responsibilities or burdens that belong to God or to my husband, my tension rises to a level that renders me frustrated and incapable of coping. Such tension quickly leads to depression. I must give up those burdens to God or to the person responsible.

I often received letters from a person whose

situation left me depressed. The depression followed me like a black cloud, dominating my life and draining my spiritual, emotional, and physical strength. One day, I just gave it up to God. Laying open the letter before Him, I said, "Lord, this is too big for me to handle. You take this problem and work in it. I cannot make anything good happen. It's all yours." The result has been freedom from the depression produced by stress that is not mine to bear.

Many women are depressed because they assume responsibility and pressure for their families that God intends husbands to carry. How we need families to demonstrate to a world with confused value systems and broken homes, the principles found in Ephesians 5: Dad assumes leadership in things spiritual as well as financial, teaching his children and loving his wife as Christ loves the church. Mom assists him by her submission and support, refusing to usurp his authority. The same pressures that cause her to be depressed can cause him to be fulfilled as a man, as he takes up the responsibility given to him by God.

When pressures of life drive us to despair, we need to recognize that God understands and turn to Him in our need. "Let us therefore draw near with confidence to the throne of grace, that we may receive mercy and may find grace to help in time of need" (Heb. 4:16).

Maybe He will give wisdom to reorganize our time and priorities or to eliminate some activities. Or He may step into the situation in a supernatural way to solve the problem as He did in Moses' case.

8

SOMETHING IN COMMON

Walking along the path of depression with our friends from ancient past, I have observed many differences among them—different circumstances, pressures, causes for their depression, and God's varied ways of meeting them in their depression. Yet there was one thing they all had in common. Each one had to arrive at a place of helplessness in his or her life, stripped of self-confidence, before God could help them.

The stories in the Old Testament illustrate truths in the New. What is the significance of each of these Old Testament characters going through a process which brought them to the end of their own resources and self-sufficiency?

We have illustrated in each of their stories the truth of John 15:5: "For without me ye can do nothing."

ILLUSTRATION OF THE TRUTH

Elijah, after running in defeat from Jezebel, came to the end of his self-sufficiency as he hid in fear in the lonely cave. At this point God spoke to Him, bringing restoration and recommissioning.

Naomi reached a point of despair in her grief where she had no ability to provide for herself. Everything was gone, and she realized it. At this lowest point in her life God moved to provide her needs, both physical and emotional. In coming to know "the God who provides," joy replaced Naomi's depression.

Jeremiah came to a place where he ministered apart from his own physical resources or any self-confidence. From divine commission to a martyr's death, his helplessness forced him to depend on God. When he focused his attention on his own inadequacy or on the suffering around him, he fell into depression. Nestling in God's protective arms of love and care, caused Jeremiah to rejoice in the midst of agonizing circumstances.

As long as Job protested his self-righteousness and protected his reputation, depression, as well as physical torture, racked his emaciating body. Seeing himself as nothing before a powerful and majestic God, released God's power in his life to bring healing and restoration.

For years Hannah wallowed in the mire of depression. She longed for a child, unable to find contentment. She and Elkanah must have tried desperately to have a baby, without suc- cess. At the temple where she gave her desire to God and made her vow, Hannah recognized her own inability to solve her problem of barren- ness. She came to the end of herself, yielding totally to the adequacy of God.

Jonah wasn't so willing to see himself filled with sin and self. He was driven to admit his helplessness as he meditated in the slimy depths of a fish's belly. Recognizing God as his only resource, he cried, "Help!" (Jonah 2:2–9). Bro- ken to some degree he obediently preached to the Ninevites. But he was again forced to admit his powerlessness to bring God's judgment on his hated enemies.

Moses no doubt came to the end of himself sometime during his experience of tending sheep in the wilderness of Midian. After at- tempting to set Israel free from oppression by his own strength and failing miserably, he re- treated to the desert, broken and defeated (Exod. 2:11–15). Forty years passed before God re- assigned Moses to the task He had all along planned for him, to lead the Israelites out of Egypt to their own land. Moses daily depended upon God, rather than himself—for the parting of the Red Sea, for water to drink and manna to eat, for deliverance from enemies. As the pressures became intolerable and Moses looked at his own inadequacy, depression followed. It served as a reminder of who he was—insufficient—and who God is—all-sufficient.

In each case, depression was the tool used to cause each person to realize the inadequacy of his or her own resources and futility of relying on self and personal abilities. Victory resulted as lives of failure and defeat were exchanged for God's life of provision and power.

THE EXPLANATION OF THE TRUTH

"Apart from me you can do nothing," Jesus told His disciples. Somehow we don't quite believe Him, as we try desperately to be good Christians, good husbands and wives, good employees, or good bosses. Struggling and striving in our own strength eventually brings failure, defeat, and depression. Is there no solution to this cycle from struggle to depression, to increased striving and deeper depression?

Jesus Christ said, "If therefore the Son shall make you free, you shall be free indeed" (John 8:36). This has to include freedom from depression, or the Word of God is untrue and there is no hope in the world. Let us look then at the path to freedom from depression through the explanation of this truth.

Judicial Explanation

It has been shown that depression is a condition of despair affecting the emotions and the mind—a symptom. As a fever indicates infection or disease, so depression acts as a thermometer to let us know something is wrong. Doctors generally are more concerned with treating the cause than with alleviating symptoms in physical illness. Likewise, God wasted no time treating the symptoms. He dealt directly with the cause, the real disease in every case, which was conclusively the self-life.

Elijah, Jeremiah, and the rest all had a problem of looking at the self in the midst of trying circumstances, rather than to God. God looked behind the symptoms of depression, seemingly even ignoring it, and confronted individuals with the problem—relying on self rather than on Him.

To destroy the strength of the self-life in one's experience is the solution to breaking the cycle of depression. Paul emphatically states the verdict upon the source of the self-life in Romans 6:6, 7, "Knowing this, that our old man is crucified with him, that the body of sin might be destroyed, that henceforth we should not serve sin. For he that is dead is freed from sin" (KJV).

Judicially for every believer, that old self which was inherited from Adam by physical birth, died with Christ and was buried. However, Paul did not stop there. "Likewise reckon ye also yourselves to be dead indeed unto sin, but alive unto God through Jesus Christ our Lord" (Rom. 6:11, KJV). We are alive in Him because we have been raised with Him.

"But God, who is rich in mercy, for his great love wherewith he loved us, Even when we were dead in sins, hath quickened us together with Christ, (by grace ye are saved;) And hath raised us up together, and made us sit together in heavenly places in Christ Jesus" (Eph. 2:4–6, KJV).

Death and resurrection is the solution to depression. Since I died to the sin of wrong reactions to circumstances, impulsive behavior, pride and self-righteousness, anger and prejudice, or whatever has brought about the emotional response of depression, I am free from its crippling power. Paul said again in Colossians 3:3, 5: "For ye are dead, and your life is hid with Christ in God. Mortify therefore your members which are upon the earth; fornication, uncleanness, inordinate affection, evil concupiscence, and covetousness, which is idolatry" (KJV).

You may be saying, "If this is true, then why am I depressed? Why is life so filled with the frustration of trying and failing?

Experiential Explanation

The death, burial, and resurrection of the believer with Jesus Christ is a fact to be appropriated by faith in each life. There is a cross, a place of death experientially, for every believer who would exchange his self-life for Christ's life.

It is a place of total surrender. Jesus Christ made this clear as He taught His disciples in preparation for His own death. "If any man will come after me, let him deny himself, and take up his cross daily, and follow me. For whosoever will save his life shall lose it: but whosoever will lose his life for my sake, the same shall save it" (Luke 9:23, 24, KJV).

Now our bodies are not nailed to the cross, but everything that is part of the self-life must be surrendered at the cross before it can be exchanged for Christ's life. Total surrender includes yielding up all rights, family, profession, goals, everything that self has become in his own strength. It basically gives God the right to make his judicial co-crucifixion with Christ an actuality in his experience; to take him to the cross.

Jesus Christ is an example of One who gave

up everything voluntarily in order to die; His equality with God, the independent exercise of His divine attributes, all His rights and privileges. He left the Garden of Gethsemane to face the cross, all rights surrendered. He willingly suffered humiliation and death (Phil. 2:5–8; John 14:10, 24; 5:19, 30; Heb. 5:7, 8). "Let this mind be in you . . ." exhorts us to have the same attitude that Christ had. The same emptying, surrendering all rights and privileges, with willingness to suffer humiliation, must precede the experiential cross of Luke 9:23, 24.

"But if it is factually true, why isn't that enough? Why all this talk about a cross for me?"

I grappled with this problem, full of questions on the outside and turmoil on the inside. If you would have asked me if I were totally surrendered to Jesus Christ, I would have answered, "Yes." Several years ago Philippians 3:10 became the desire of my heart. "That I may know him, and the power of his resurrection, and the followship of his sufferings, being made conformable unto his death" (Phil. 3:10, KJV). "Even suffering, Lord, just let me know you," I prayed.

However, when confronted with the truth of my need to enter into my death with Christ experientially, I was struck with the fact that I had not totally surrendered. I was still bound by crippling emotions and fears. God ran a verse

through my mind like a needle stuck on a record. "Except a corn of wheat fall into the ground
and die, it abideth alone: but if it die, it bringeth
forth much fruit" (John 12:24, KJV).

I knew I had to die. But I didn't want to die!
Finally, with much struggle and pain, I laid myself on the altar, totally giving God permission
to take me to the cross. God began to reveal to
me just how He saw me. I was not any better
than the woman at the well, or Mary Magdalene.
It was only His divine protection that kept me
from living out my nature. I saw that the cross
was the only answer and I visualized "setting my
face toward Jerusalem."

Then came Gethsemane. God stripped me of
all confidence in my abilities. He revealed all the
bondage to fear and insecurity. I could see only
my helplessness and look to "Jesus, the author
and perfecter of faith, who for the joy set before Him endured the cross, despising the
shame, and has sat down at the right hand of the
throne of God" (Heb. 12:2).

I wished someone could have taken me bodily
to the cross, nailing my hands and feet. But I
knew that wasn't necessary, because He had already died in my place. I was paralyzed with
fear!

It is a work of the Holy Spirit. The Holy Spirit
must reveal to the individual the reality of his
identification with the death, burial, and res-

urrection of Jesus Christ. Intellectual understanding is only the beginning of a process which is culminated as the Holy Spirit convinces of the truth of the fact.

"But as it is written, Eye hath not seen, nor ear heard, neither have entered into the heart of man, the things which God hath prepared for them that love him. But God hath revealed them unto us by his Spirit: for the Spirit searcheth all things, yea, the deep things of God" (I Cor. 2:9, 10, KJV).

After reaching the point of total surrender, giving God permission to make real the truth of my death in Him on the cross, He completed this stage of His work in me. I saw in a moment the reality of a precious truth.

My childhood and teenage years were filled with fear and feelings of worthlessness and rejection. I built a thick wall around the real me to protect those fragile feelings, so easily hurt. But carrying it all into my adult life, I still tried to keep tight control over my emotions and protect myself. I had developed a facade of independence and adequacy and had indeed become a capable person. But inside, the old fears haunted and insecurity frequently raised its ugly head.

The fact of my death, burial, and resurrection with Christ was presented as truth, and I believed it because the Word teaches it so clearly.

"But it doesn't mean anything!" I exclaimed in great frustration.

Then suddenly a veil drew back from over my eyes and I saw that when I received eternal life, God's life, with no beginning and no ending, I inherited in Him a new history. I could exchange my life as a child for His life as a child. I could replace my memory bank, all locked up with a sign on the door, "Keep Out," for His memory bank. I was free, and for the first time I was a little girl loved by my heavenly Father.

This new insight was not the end, but only the beginning of a new life, of Christ's life in me as God conforms me to the image of Christ.

A letter from a friend described this revelation of the Spirit to her this way.

Yesterday for the first time I understood what it means to "reckon myself also to be dead indeed unto sin, but alive unto God through Jesus Christ my Lord." I'm so excited by this new light that I all but split my cheeks with a continuous smile today.

She went on to tell of months of struggle to understand and her continuous defeat, and then continued.

Yesterday I studied Romans 6 and the Holy Spirit just opened my eyes and heart to His

Word, which is "sharper than a two-edged sword." Since then I have several times counted on this truth and have seen God work. It is true and I don't have to give in to my old response-habits.

APPLICATION OF THE TRUTH

Understanding both judicially and experientially the believer's death, burial, and resurrection with Christ is the key to victory over depression. At the cross the self-life dominated by depression is exchanged for Christ's life. We are raised with Him to heavenly places. Everything that is Christ's life is now my life—love, joy, peace, and whatever I need to face life's frustrations and difficulties. The stranglehold of depression over the emotions is broken under the tremendous resurrection power of Jesus Christ (Eph. 1:18–23).

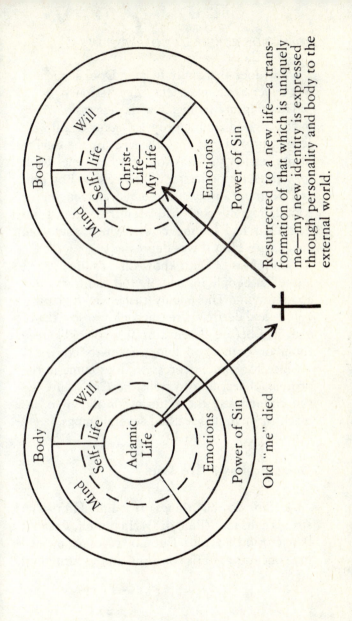

Resurrected to a new life—a transformation of that which is uniquely me—my new identity is expressed through personality and body to the external world.

Old "me" died

How does this apply to me? Does it mean I will never again experience depression?

Thinking my struggles with depression were over for good after appropriating my death with Jesus Christ, I was not prepared for the deluge of depression that was to overwhelm me. I felt friendless, misunderstood, and rejected by others. Nothing in my life seemed challenging or stimulating; my goals had been frustrated; I felt that God had let me down, which made me angry with Him. I was depressed!

Where was I? Did I know Christ's life at all? I looked at people instead of God and found disappointment. The enemy rushed in to harass, defeat, and destroy. I reached a lower low than I ever had before. I heard Satan's voice, like the sound of soothing oil, tempting me to "cop out."

Since for some, depression does come in the process of learning to walk the Christ-life, we can either waste the suffering or allow God to teach through it. I learned several things.

God's Promises Are True

"I can do all things through Him who strengthens me" (Phil. 4:13). In myself, I cannot be victorious in trials. But God cares for me and my concerns are His concerns. In the turmoil of problems I had forgotten that and turned against Him.

One day, after some of the fury of negative emotions subsided, God reminded me of His love and care. "Vivian, don't you remember? It is I in you and you in me. One step at a time, we'll take care of the problems."

I confessed my anger and sin against God, and although circumstances didn't change, my attitude did, bringing me the peace I needed.

God Demands First Priority

God allowed me the opportunity to pour out my feelings to Him. At times when I couldn't stand the depths of my despair, He gave me someone to listen and understand. Yet He taught me afresh the futility of looking to people or projects for security and satisfaction instead of to Him. He brought me to a place again, of crying out from my heart, "Nothing else matters but you, God. I'll cling to you regardless of my feelings or people or circumstances."

Self-acceptance Essential

God reminded me that He made me with my personality for a reason. He planned that chord that causes my soul to vibrate—my temperament. I thought of the words, "Can a leopard change his spots?" Or, "Can the clay say to the potter, 'Why have you made me this way?'"

My weakness toward depression is the other side of a creative temperament that God has planned for His glory. Rather than struggle against this weakness, which only magnifies it, I must accept this part of me, for then I can know the truth of II Corinthians 12:9. "'My grace is sufficient for you, for power is perfected in weakness'. Most gladly, therefore, I will rather boast about my weaknesses, that the power of Christ may dwell in me." Victory over depression is not in my own strength or because of my efforts to thwart its control in my life, but only in Jesus Christ.

We Are Involved in a Spiritual Warfare

Sometimes when everything goes well, we forget that "we wrestle not against flesh and blood, but against principalities, against powers, against the rulers of the darkness of this world, against spiritual wickedness in high places" (Eph. 6:12, KJV).

I have become more aware of the subtlety and strength of the enemy. Satan took every advantage to beat and oppress me when I was already down. I could see his heinous intent to destroy and block God's purpose in my life There were times when I could do nothing but rely on someone else's prayer. I have felt like the recipient of Christ's words to Peter: "Vivian, Vivian, Satan has desired to sift you as wheat. But I have prayed for you. . . ."

Accept the Circumstances

Struggling against unpleasant circumstances only increases depression. I came to an acceptance of the valley of troubles through which I was passing, understanding that growth comes in stages—sometimes painfully. I saw myself as a piece of clay on God's potter's wheel, knowing that His loving hands shaped the vessel. He allowed only the pressure needed to mold me into the shape He desired. Resting in this truth, I had the confidence that joy would return after the trial had accomplished its work.

God Teaches Through Suffering

At one point toward the end of these cataclysmic pressures, I had reached a new point of despair. Because of distorted emotions, I believed I was incapable of receiving or giving love. Many years of my life had been spent seeking for freedom, only to be given a taste and have it elude my grasp.

Finally after the "fire and the wind and the

earthquake" of previous weeks, I heard the voice of gentle stillness.

"Vivian, why do you search for what is already yours? Christ in you is Love: therefore you have love, you do love; just believe it."

I stopped in my tracks! "God, is that you?"

The truth was confirmed from I John as I read: "Beloved, let us love one another, for love is from God: and every one who loves is born of God and knows God.... By this the love of God was manifested in us, that God sent His only begotten Son into the world so that we might live through Him.... If we love one another, God abides in us, and His love is perfected in us" (4:7–12).

I could stop searching for what was already mine and just begin to believe it and act on it! God had revealed the indwelling Christ to me in a new way. Joy replaced depression!

A FEW FINAL THOUGHTS

The continual underlying depressiveness that haunted me daily is gone. The sense of hopelessness in ever knowing victory has disappeared. "For the law of the Spirit of life in Christ Jesus hath made me free from the law of sin and death" (Rom. 8:2, KJV). The law of a depressive

response in my life leading to, and often result-ing from, sin, no longer binds me. In Christ Jesus, the law of the Spirit of life controls me and I am free!

But I have a choice daily, to walk after the flesh, or according to the life of the Holy Spirit in me. "This I say then, Walk in the Spirit, and ye shall not fulfill the lust of the flesh" (Gal. 5:16, KJV).

Paul makes it very clear in Romans 6 that since I died with Christ, I am to count it a fact and daily yield myself to God as an instrument for righteousness. He further explains victory in Romans 8. Notice verse 6: "For to be carnally minded is death; but to be spiritually minded is life and peace" (KJV).

Paul is saying that if we set our minds on the things of this world, the result is destruction in our lives. But to set our minds on the things of the Spirit is life and peace in daily experience. I must choose with my will to set my mind on the things of God—my acceptance in Jesus Christ, His beautiful qualities, promises of the Word, continuously being in communion with Him. The mind set on the Spirit is life and peace—free from depression.

Nevertheless, we will not reach, in this life, the perfection waiting for us when we see Jesus Christ face to face. Therefore, we may fall occa-

sionally into the trap of thinking incorrectly, re lying on our own strength rather than exclu sively God's, and become depressed. How do we deal with it?

1. We need to understand that depression is a symptom, *usually* resulting from the "self-life" or "walking after the flesh," which is always inadequate to deal with specific precipitating circumstances.

2. At the first hint of the downward pull of negative emotions we must remind ourselves that an old recording is about to play, that "flesh" is attempting to gain control and cause defeat.

3. Thank God for our own weakness in dealing with the problem. See circumstances as an opportunity for God to demonstrate His strength. "For when I am weak, then I am strong" (II Cor. 12:10).

4. Focus our attention on the faithful character of God, as revealed in Jesus Christ who is our life. Rebellion, anxiety, lack of trust, anger against God, must be confessed and His forgiveness received.

5. Remember that we are involved in a spiritual warfare, and that Satan is our adversary, who, "as a roaring lion, walketh about, seeking whom he may devour" (I Peter 5:8, KJV). Remember too, that our victory is already accomplished in Jesus Christ (Eph. 1:18–22).

6. When physical illness or hormone imbalance is involved, proper medical advice is necessary, as well as accepting patiently the suffering as allowed by a loving Father for His purpose and our ultimate good.

7. Sometimes when the depression is due to a physical problem, Satanic oppression, or we just don't see any reason for the emotional down, we need to "float" with the feelings. That is, agree to have the emotions temporarily, remembering that "underneath are the everlasting arms," and wait for God to reveal what He desires in the situation.

James 1:2–4 says, "My brethren, count it all joy when ye fall into divers temptations; Knowing this, that the trying of your faith worketh patience. But let patience have her perfect work, that ye may be perfect and entire, wanting nothing" (KJV). God, the Master Sculptor, desires to perfect and complete us, that we might become like Jesus Christ. He shapes and chips off rough edges and defects, until one day we stand, a finished sculpture, a beautiful work of art, in His image. Sometimes depression assumes the shape of a chisel in God's hand. When its work is accomplished, He throws away the tool.

Are you depressed? Do you know someone who is depressed? I hope you have learned to know and walk with the God of Elijah, Naomi, Jeremiah, Job, Hannah, Jonah, and Moses—the

God who comforts, encourages, confronts, forgives, instructs, and helps. I trust you will learn to appropriate all you are and have in Jesus Christ; to know the joy of the indwelling Holy Spirit; to sing a song of praise, triumphant over depression.

"Therefore if any man be in Christ, he is a new creature: old things are passed away; behold, all things are become new" (II Cor. 5:17, KJV).